STARDUST DANCING

A SEEKER'S GUIDE TO THE MIRACULOUS

Paul Tobolowsky, M.D.

DEDICATION

To June and Dave,
To Deborah, Mark, and Andrew,
To Barbie and Stephen,
But mostly to Judy, to Judy, to Judy

ACKNOWLEDGMENTS

I don't know how transformative revelations happen, but I feel fortunate to have experienced such a revelation. As I discussed my vision with a group of friends, some gave me so much encouragement to write this book that it eventually became easier to write it than to not write it. Special thanks in that regard go to Dr. David Alkek, Bennett Litwin, Dr. Tom Hampton, Rob Olson, Jack Youngkin, and Bob Berman.

When I had completed the manuscript and wanted to turn it into a published book, Liz Conrad Goedecke not only provided the wonderful cover art and design, but also, with her boundless positive energy, played a big role in organizing the book's final form. Digital artist and photographer, Larry P. Ammann, (www.RemoteSensingArt.com) contributed the background cover starscape. Editor David Farnham was of great assistance in helping me say twice as much in half as many words. The cover photo of the author was taken by Judy Tobolowsky. The author possesses many albums of Judy's photos, featuring their three amazing children and the experiences of a wonderful life together.

For their gracious cover reviews, I thank Dr. Larry Dossey, Dr. Gilbert Cuthbertson, Reverend Fred Durham, and Dr. Bonnie Jacobs. Dr. Jacobs in addition was kind enough to write the Foreword.

My career as a medical doctor allowed me to meet some wonderful people, who continually inspired me and helped me see how miraculous life can be. I hope those patients recognize what they have meant to me through the words of this book.

In addition to taking the cover photo of the author, Judy Tobolowsky contributed to the book in many other ways. She co-edited it, compiled the endnotes and bibliography, assisted with word selection, and provided much-needed wisdom and support. The freedom of self-publishing this book allows me to admit that I love Judy Tobolowsky and always will.

Paul Tobolowsky, M.D.

CONTENTS

FOREWORD

We are in need of a book like *Stardust Dancing* right now, and I'm very glad Dr. Tobolowsky has written it. I hope that everyone will enjoy this book as much as I did. Readers will find that Dr. Tobolowsky's deep and broad understanding of science is what informs his views on the wonders of life and the natural world. In fact, it is the interconnectedness of all of life to both the living and non-living parts of Earth and the universe – that he finds "miraculous."

What I love about this book is Dr. Tobolowsky's approach to explaining exactly why we should all be just as joyful as he is when we too understand things such as the nature of DNA, the fueling of our bodies with food, our chemical connection to the very origin of the universe, and other natural phenomena. Dr. Tobolowsky implores us to become aware, and to try and remain aware, of the wondrous nature of our own selves. As he says: "More valuable than a million lifeless galaxies is the living consciousness that is you."

Every one of us has neurons, inner ears, eyes, and taste buds that work in truly marvelous ways. True, our mammalian relatives share these traits, but humans have the unique ability to seek understanding of the processes of life and to view our lives with awe. In fact, Dr. Tobolowsky brings an interesting philosophical discussion to bear on the biology of our senses, by pointing out that we do not simply perceive what is already there in the outside world. Our sensory organs provide us with a unique interpretation of what is around us: "…to consider our sensory experiences as interactions rather than 'me' perceiving 'it' changes our relationship with the world and knits us into its tapestry. We and the outside world are parts of the recipe for every sensory interaction, both equally necessary for that sensory experience to occur, co-creators."

As a scientist, I often forget how remarkable the world and we really are – especially in the larger context of our place in nature (including the universe). But, this book, approximately equal parts information and inspiration – never fails to lift my spirits. When next confronted with or disheartened by violence, spite, or the mundane, I will do my best to remember Dr. Tobolowsky's words: "It does not seem possible that we could exist, but in our world, nothing is commoner than the seemingly impossible."

Dr. Bonnie F. Jacobs
Associate Professor of Earth Sciences
Roy M. Huffington Department of Earth Sciences
Southern Methodist University
Dallas, Texas

RIDDLES, DISGUISES, AND BURNING BUSHES

Arnold: "Murray, I finally figured out your problem. There's only one thing that really bothers you ... Other people. If it wasn't for them other people, everything would be great, huh, Murray? I mean, you think everything's fine, and then you go out into the street ... and there they all *are* again, right? The Other People; taking up space, bumping into you, asking for things, making lines to wait on, taking cabs away from ya ... The Enemy ... Well, *watch* out, Murray, they're *everywhere* ..."

Herb Gardner
A Thousand Clowns

"In *that* direction," the [Cheshire] Cat said, waving its right paw round, "lives a Hatter: and in *that* direction," waving the other paw, "lives a March Hare. Visit either you like: they're both mad."
"But I don't want to go among mad people," Alice remarked.
"Oh, you can't help that," said the Cat: "we're all mad here. I'm mad. You're mad."
"How do you know I'm mad?" said Alice.
"You must be," said the Cat, "or you wouldn't have come here."

Lewis Carroll
Alice's Adventures in Wonderland

Margaret: "What is the victory of a cat on a hot tin roof? - I wish I knew ... Just staying on it, I guess, as long as she can ..."

Tennessee Williams
Cat on a Hot Tin Roof

13

Riddle

Let me give you a riddle that sounds like a trick question. First, imagine everything in the world that ever existed. For example, imagine a pond or pile of mud in the ancient days of Earth and a one-celled organism moving through it. Imagine a sandal worn on the left foot of Emperor Nero, Julius Caesar, or some long-forgotten citizen of the Roman Empire. Picture a cloud sweeping across the sky above Europe or South America one afternoon 12 centuries ago, or a weed growing in a nondescript field in the year 1502 or 1826. Think about the countless living and non-living forms that ever existed.

Now consider every event that ever happened - the steps taken by Nero in his sandals, field workers pausing for a moment in the shade of the cloud centuries ago, the weed growing in spring rains before succumbing to late summer drought. This brings me to my riddle: When you sum up every event that ever happened to everything that ever existed, what do you get?

You get your own existence! You get the world just as it is at this moment.

The world is its own adding machine, taking as input its past, and generating from that input a brand new alignment of ingredients every instant. One of the undeniable features of the current moment is the living conscious presence of you. Every ancient mud puddle and one-celled organism, every sandaled step taken in the Roman Empire, every cloud and weed in the history of the world contributed to the current order, and therefore to the creation of you. Look anywhere and you will discover other forms that the entire history of the world has generated.

To take it a step further, the planet Earth could not have the history that it does were it not part of a universe whose laws, energy, and atoms have led to your creation. It is, in fact, the entire universe that is summed at each moment, and part of that sum right now is You. For your explorations, you have been granted a body with thousands of miles of blood vessels and a brain with more nerve connections than the number of galaxies in the observable universe.

The world continues to generate clouds and mud puddles, catfish and armadillos. Each of these forms is part of the answer to my riddle, part of the sum of all world history each moment reveals. *Think about the amazing truth that everything that ever happened in the history of the world resulted in your own life at this moment!* Look outside at a cloud or a flower or another person that likewise reflects the sum of all history. Think what this moment represents, and what you represent. Calmly await the next moment, when the world will again sum up its total history and reveal it to you and through you.

Introduction to You

I will tell you the single greatest truth about yourself. Your very existence as a living conscious human being is astounding. Every atom in your body was once an inanimate part of the planet Earth or its atmosphere. These atoms that now pump within your heart or capture light in your eyes existed long before your birth, and are in fact *billions* of years old! They have been gathered from around the galaxy and been part of many other forms and processes through the eons before becoming part of you. Within you these ancient atoms have been brought to life and ultimately to consciousness. This very day you added additional atoms to your body by dining on the elements of the planet and inhaling its air, transmuting cosmic ingredients into You.

Yet we generally do not feel so miraculous as we go through life. It is easy to perceive ourselves as vulnerable isolated individuals caught in a web of stresses and sorrows. How do such remarkable beings lose awareness of their magnificence?

What is a Miracle?

The *American Heritage Dictionary of the English Language* begins its definition of the word "miracle" in the customary way: "An event that appears unexplainable by the laws of nature ..." [1] Let us stretch and twist the definition somewhat. If an extremely improbable event not only happens, but happens often, would that constitute a miracle? For example, if the ball falls into slot number 24 on an honest roulette wheel 30 times in a row, would that be considered miraculous? If the atoms of dirt become living organisms, would that qualify?

At what point does the occurrence - and subsequent reoccurrence - of an apparently improbable event cross the threshold of what we would consider miraculous? What if essentially everything about You crosses that threshold?

You are the roulette wheel in which the ball lands in the "survive" slot every moment of your life. You are the atoms of dirt that become beating hearts, nerve networks that think, and bones whose rigid exterior provides protection and support while their delicate interior marrow produces blood cells. Yet despite the thousands of processes your body is performing at this moment to sustain your existence, the dictionary will not credit you with being miraculous unless you start breaking scientific laws.

This, of course, you cannot do. No matter what happens, no matter how many near-impossibilities pave the trail to you, science will accommodate. If new discoveries break old scientific "laws," science adapts by tossing out the old laws and creating new provisional theories that incorporate the new findings. This is often the way science advances. From your debut as a single cell, through your development into a body with a mind and a heart and trillions of specialized interacting cells that keep each other alive, hardly anything about you seems rationally plausible. *Logically, you should not exist.*

Surely the string of implausibilities that constitutes your life can only be viewed as miraculous. Toss out your dictionary for being so narrow and unimaginative in its definition. Look at the planet you inhabit; look at yourself. My task is easy – I only need to tell you the truth.

Science Fiction

Imagine a science fiction story about an amazing planet. Imagine that the planet's surface coalesces into living organisms, some of which attach to the planet while others move around relatively freely. On this planet, plants stick roots down into the ground to transport upward the precise elements that they need to form themselves. This already sounds far-fetched. Then imagine that the planet orbits a star almost 100 million miles away, yet its plants capture the energy of this star's light and use it to bring their collection of chemicals to life. Picture other organisms ingesting the plants, turning the plant's atoms into their own atoms. Think of a vast array of living beings transmuting the planet's soil into roots, stems, eyes, ears, emotions.

To pile incredulity upon incredulity, allow every life form to contain a genetic blueprint so that organisms of its kind thousands of years in the future will arise to carry out this same alchemy. Over time, some absolutely improbable organisms on the planet take one giant leap farther and, through their consciousness, develop the intellectual capacity to ponder their own existence.

This story is so implausible that it would likely be rejected as science fiction, but it is of course the actual saga of our Earth. It is also our individual history as transient forms channeling this cosmic process into our life, our thoughts, and our passions. But this is not the narrative we learn about ourselves or our world. Rather we are taught from birth a series of interwoven story lines in which we are expected to take part. We root for the local football team, struggle in business, worry about the future, experience joy and pain through our relationships, and are informed (often via mass media) who our heroes and villains are. We find ourselves either an active character or helpless pawn in the stresses of each story that we incorporate into our own personal narrative. Certainly these themes are part of our life journey, but we are myopic if they become all that we see.

Each culture has its own set of rules by which life is to be "played" and what qualifies as a win. All these themes block our view of the continuing set of miracles through which we exist.

Regardless of football losses or business downturns, through us the universe is brought to life.

Don't let others pick which story lines matter to you, and don't automatically accept from the culture around you how the narrative of your life will be defined. The power to define yourself belongs to you. Pick the bigger, more expansive story in which to cast yourself.

We are not just the storyteller; we are the story that we tell.

The Case of the Purloined Miracles

As in an old-fashioned detective yarn, we have a mystery to solve. There was a time described in ancient holy traditions when miracles seemed commonplace, but not anymore. Where did they go? In the movie version, on a pier on a foggy night, a seedy character in a trench coat would walk past you whispering that the miracles were hidden, not stolen, before he vanished into the night.

Although the original perpetrator of the miracles' disappearance remains murky, the composite police sketch of the accomplice looks a lot like each of us. At the very least, we have been less than zealous in trying to track down the missing miracles. It isn't our fault. Misled by the testimony of seemingly trustworthy witnesses, we have gone off on wild goose chases. We have been distracted by deceptions, duped by disguises. Some of the deceptions and disguises have been quite alluring, and we have perhaps been smitten by them.

There has in fact been an inadvertent conspiracy, a cover-up in which we unknowingly participated. Here are some of the concepts behind which the miracles have been hidden.

The Three Pigs

No less a cultural authority than my brother has agreed with a number of evolutionary biologists in trying to explain our focus on the Negative. If one caveman obsessed about the dangers of marauding elephants while his less neurotic neighbor thought they were cute, perhaps the worrier might be more likely to hide, survive, mate, and pass genetically onward these anxiety-laden tendencies. Along with this genetic predisposition came parent to child teachings in support of a worldview that we live surrounded by varying hierarchies of danger.

With this story as a life theme, we accept the stress that accompanies a focus on the Negative, presuming that therein lies safety. According to this theory, even our memory is skewed. Presumably, our ancient ancestors were more likely to survive if their memory of charging mastodons remained acute, reducing their risk of exposing themselves in the future to those dangers they faced in the past.

Regardless of whether this view of a threatening world has an evolutionary basis, it is certainly embedded in our psyche. A silly but useful example of the indoctrination we received as children can be found in the story, "The Three Pigs." Many of us watched the tale as a Walt Disney cartoon featuring a happy ending, with a catchy theme song ("Who's Afraid of the Big Bad Wolf?"), though there are many earlier (and darker) versions of the story.

We initially follow the antics of two immature little pigs who simply want to spend their days dancing and singing, enjoying the moment, unconcerned with safeguarding their futures. They build flimsy houses out of straw and sticks, scant protection, acceptable for fair weather but not built with adequate concern for potential future adversity. The hero of this tale is the diligent third pig who sweats to build a house of bricks, sacrificing the pleasures of the moment for greater eventual security. After all, the third pig presumes that the world is a dangerous place.

Sure enough, along comes adversity in the form of The Big Bad Wolf, who would have devoured Pigs One and Two had they not been saved by finding shelter in the brick house of Pig Number Three. Sacrifice on the part of the dutiful third pig is rewarded, the folly of living for the moment is exposed, and the dangerous, carnivorous nature of the outside world revealed.

A different culture, viewing life through a less jittery prism, might have come up with an alternative ending. Perhaps the wolf, instead of attacking the pigs, moved out of the neighborhood or reformed, allowing even the devil-may-care pigs to live to a ripe old age. Then the loser would have been the curmudgeonly Pig Number Three, who toiled away the days of his life wasting anxiety on hypothetical threats while his compadres were having a jolly time. The third pig might then have quoted the French essayist Montaigne: "My life has been filled with terrible misfortune; most of which never happened." [2] Or perhaps a flood could have tragically wiped out the whole bunch, in which case Pigs One and Two at least experienced some merriment in their brief lives.

As we sat on our parent's knee listening to this story, we certainly were not aware that we were learning a worldview. In fact, our parents probably weren't aware that they were indoctrinating us, but saw themselves as merely telling a cute fairytale. Yet such stories are passed on because they harmonize with something intrinsic to the culture, leaving the child not only entertained but also a step closer to membership into that society.

News coverage feeds into the negative bias of this worldview. There are many menaces, new ones every day, and yesterday's protections no longer bring security. A house of bricks protects against wolves, so it isn't completely worthless, but more potent dangers surround us, rendering mere bricks inadequate to safeguard what we hold dear. Every time we hear or read the latest news, the same ancient emotional buttons are pressed with the newest incarnations of The Big Bad Wolf.

I do not challenge that we exist among hierarchies of threats. I do challenge that story as the appropriate theme of our lives. Our very existence is a miracle. Every person we meet is likewise a miracle. Every conversation we hold with another human being is a miracle. The Earth, with its ability to generate life, is a miracle. Every bird and blade of grass is a miracle. Each day provides the opportunity to explore our miraculous nature.

Without denying that threats exist and are part of life, without denying that sorrow is likewise part of the human experience, this curtain of life as a series of perils must be pulled back if we are to see the miracles on the other side. The path to amazement is everywhere, and in a sense you already know it. Instead of collecting fears, try collecting miracles. After all, miracles are weightless and don't take up any space, so you can keep collecting them your entire life and your pockets will still have room for more.

South Indian Monkey Trap

In his book *Zen and the Art of Motorcycle Maintenance* (which was reputedly rejected for publication 121 times), brilliant and reclusive American author Robert Pirsig describes the South Indian Monkey Trap. [3] The "machinery" for the trap is a hollowed-out coconut staked to the ground. To bait the trap, the villagers poke a hole in the coconut, and partially fill it with rice.

Along comes the monkey, lured by the rice, reaching through the hole into the coconut to grasp the delectable dinner on the inside. But the hole through which he reaches into the coconut is just barely large enough for the monkey to insert his empty hand. When his fist is full of rice, it becomes too large to withdraw from the hole. The monkey is trapped, unable to remove his rice-filled hand. And yet, what is really trapping the monkey? He has been lured to the trap by his value system that exalts the acquisition of rice. His parents, his peers, his entire lifetime experience all support this value judgment, and all these witnesses seem credible. But now the quest for rice is imprisoning him. There is no mechanism within the coconut that is holding him; he is trapped entirely by his values. All he has to do to become free is to realize that at this moment the quest for rice is depriving him of his freedom. If he simply lets go of the rice, he can extract his hand and walk away. Yet the monkey, unable to re-evaluate his priorities, continues trying unsuccessfully to extricate his fist full of rice from the coconut. Eventually the villagers come along to round up the captured monkeys.

Those must really be stupid monkeys, don't you think? Yet Pirsig's analogy serves to remind us, not of the foolishness of monkeys, but of the potential of a value system to entrap. Anyone who currently feels caught in his present lifestyle need only ask himself what is trapping him. Perhaps outside forces or physical disabilities are the culprits, greatly limiting one's opportunities. However, the average person undoubtedly helps create his own trap with his values. We want certain things from life and reach out our hand to grab those things. We design our schedule to achieve these priorities of our own choosing. Then we hold ourselves to a self-imposed program in hopes of grasping these goals. For a person who feels hopelessly ensnared in an unhappy lifestyle, it is perhaps surprising to realize that it is not necessarily the world out there that is applying the trap. Like the monkeys, we need to re-evaluate whether the quest for apparently desirable goals might be depriving us of our freedom.

Of course, we become trapped, not only by our material desires, but by all our desires. The quest for prestige, for friendship or love, for power or control, likewise imprisons us. But "life" does not force us to seek what we seek; we make these choices ourselves, though we do not make them in a vacuum. The world over, each individual lives immersed in a culture that constantly displays its set of values. By observing his culture, a Norwegian learns how to be a Norwegian, and a Tibetan how to be a Tibetan. He learns what to desire, what to value.

Even in a free society like ours, it is remarkable that most people choose variants of the same lifestyle. We eat similar kinds of meals, enjoy similar entertainments, pursue similar ambitions. Technology plays a growing role in letting developed societies know who its heroes and villains are, what the rungs are on the ladder of success, and even what is fashionable to wear on the journey. As we reach for what we value, we don't necessarily give a great deal of independent analysis to the artificial source of this worldview. The set of values seems like truth itself. Like the South Indian monkeys, we reach for what we value without critical consideration of its cost.

Our culture prizes ambition. What we lack becomes a seductive temptress, leading us to devalue what we currently have. Hence we reach for more and more, and each grasp traps our hand. This worldview is yet another curtain that must be peeled away to reveal the realm of miracles. Rice is not hidden, but rains down upon us.

Can anything set us free? Yes, we can let go of the rice in any particular coconut, pull our hand out, and we are free. It can be done in a moment, any moment, this moment. Choose your coconuts wisely.

Roles

Ram Dass, Harvard professor, LSD researcher, and lifelong mystic, tells a joke that is not meant for hilarity. A man enters the shop of a well-respected tailor to have a new suit made. The tailor takes measurements and makes the suit. When the man returns to try it on, he finds that the sleeves are the wrong length and there is too much material in the back. Disturbed, the man asks the tailor to perform alterations.

Instead, the tailor tells the man to twist his back, contort his shoulders, and lean to one side as he walks, which makes the suit appear to fit as long as the man stands in that twisted posture. Holding himself at these awkward angles, the man leaves the shop. Two onlookers are standing outside the store; one remarks to the other that only a brilliant tailor like this one could achieve a perfect fit on such a deformed man.

Ram Dass says that he himself has been that man, and so are we. We each acquire roles that aren't such a perfect match for us, requiring a twist of the shoulder here and a hunch of the back there. Our lives seem like a good fit - as long as we are willing to remain contorted. As we take on roles, we become identified with those roles, and often come to think of the roles as our real self. Simultaneously we reinforce the roles played by others, likewise recognizing them as real. So we soldier on, backs hunched and listing to one side or the other. To some extent, we are all in disguise.

The solution, Ram Dass points out, is to seek out our deeper self that over the course of our personal history has adopted those roles. If we can access this deeper consciousness that exists beyond any roles, we can slip roles on and off as we wish, "like a glove." [4] We can then free ourselves from the trap each role creates. We must take off our own disguise if we are to appreciate the miracle that we really are beneath the roles that we portray.

Certainly, some roles are worth keeping, even if they require major hunching and twisting. These are choices we each must make. However, the freedom to choose is ours. We must pick our roles wisely; we do not want to become the unknowing servant of our roles.

"Shared Illusions"

"When we look closely, we find many of the assumptions of modern society are based ... on shared illusions." [5] So states physicist Leonard Mlodinow in The Drunkard's Walk. It can be difficult to tell illusion from truth, particularly when great masses of people share a particular belief. "Human perception," Mlodinow paraphrases 19th century scientist Michael Faraday, "is not a direct consequence of reality but rather an act of imagination." [6]

When we have a belief, we don't search for ways to prove it wrong - we try to prove it right. This is called confirmation bias, which leads us to integrate new information to support pre-existing beliefs. Mlodinow quotes Sir Francis Bacon (considered by many to be the creator of the scientific method) from the year 1620: "... the human understanding, once it has adopted an opinion, collects any instances that confirm it, and though the contrary instances may be more numerous and more weighty, it either does not notice them or else rejects them, in order that this opinion will remain unshaken." [7]

Human beings are quite adept at putting events into patterns. We awaken each day, not with a blank slate for interpreting new events, but to a world of pre-existing passions, conflicts, and strong shared belief systems. The patterns we perceive today are dictated by the way we - and our culture - perceived patterns in the past. Mlodinow suggests that to see the world more clearly and free ourselves from the confirmation bias, we need to question rather than blindly accept our existing interpretations. He advises, "... we should learn to spend as much time looking for evidence that we are wrong as we spend searching for reasons we are correct." [8]

However, the emotional centers of our brain give us positive reinforcement when we comply with the pre-existing shared beliefs of our society. In particular, brain connections involving an area called the orbitofrontal cortex activate positive emotional circuitry and a sense of reward when cultural mores are followed. This is true regardless of a person's culture, though different societies view "truth" differently. We are programmed neurologically and emotionally to seek and obtain membership in our own culture by accepting its assumptions. These assumptions usually come as a "package deal."

Who are your society's allies and who are its enemies? Did you make these decisions for yourself, or did you learn the answers through acculturation? What constitutes a successful life? Did you make your own decision on this? If you live on a small island, you are likely respected based on your skills as a fisherman. To what extent is your society's viewpoint absolute truth? Might part of the "package deal" represent merely a point of view?

It is one of the tenets of post-modernist philosophy that there is no such thing as a true history. An uncountable number of events happens every day, so the mere choice of what to include in an account of history introduces a selection bias. You don't have to include falsehoods to bias a historical account. I could make a video of my basketball exploits and show only my successful shots (that would require extensive editing), using true events to construct a false implication that I was a magnificent basketball player.

By choosing how to connect history's dots, a point of view is substituted for a true history. Every culture connects the dots differently, and then displays this construction as "truth." If the story line consists of events that are individually true, the bias in their selection and the way they are interwoven into a worldview may not be evident. The support of a belief system by the rest of the people in a community - be it jungle or desert island or urban metropolis - adds further credence to the independent reality of these man-made stories. To the extent that you accept a point of view as absolute truth, you participate in a "shared illusion." These illusions are difficult to identify and escape, particularly if the facts or events of the story are true, but their selection for inclusion in a particular narrative is biased. Every accurate shot I made in my hypothetical basketball video was a true event, but created a false narrative by leaving out the missed shots.

There is no more effective defense of a false or one-sided premise than the biased selection of true facts to support it. All story lines require editing, and thereby empower the editor.

I once met a psychologist who said his mission was to create reality. By this he meant that he helped clients with problems like depression or anxiety develop more uplifting story lines for their lives. The story lines would not be fiction because they had to include true life events. However, the links between events and the relative emphasis allotted allowed more than one interpretation, and he tried to help his clients find valid positive interpretations.

Advocates of a belief system, be it personal, political, or religious, often argue that their belief could not have survived this long were it not true. Obviously this is not the case. For example, if any one political or religious viewpoint is true, all conflicting viewpoints must be false, despite their long histories. If a belief cannot be proved false, and its adherents perpetuate the belief, then any belief can survive.

Conflicting beliefs lay the groundwork for a conflicted world. Documentation of this can be found in every edition of every newspaper. If you seek to combat this negativity by trying to change the world, you are challenging a formidable opponent that dwarfs you.

Adherents of shared illusions will eagerly seek your support, but you have a great untapped power, the ability to define the universe for yourself. When you play basketball, you must follow rules set by others. There are rules about scoring, and what constitutes victory, and you don't get to change those rules because they don't suit you. On the other hand, in your own life you get to choose what to value, and one of the grand prizes is the realization that you are free to make that very choice. You even get to decide how to keep score. Your worldview must be based on truth – your happiness cannot depend on blizzards in July, and you probably cannot be king of the world.

Be wary of blindly accepting "shared illusions," of yielding to others the right to set the values of your own life. Shake off their grip on you and feel your own freedom and power. Deciding what matters to you is not a one-time experience, but rather an ongoing gift that will remain yours forever.

Goose in a Bottle

I will tell two versions of a Zen riddle. In the modern version, an extremely wealthy man consults a Zen master. Despite his wealth, the rich man says he cannot find happiness or contentment. "Name your price," he asks, "and I will gladly pay it if you can teach me the secret of happiness."

"Very well," says the Zen master. "I will charge you one million dollars a day."

The rich man agrees to the terms and is given a riddle.

"Solve this, and you will find contentment," says the master. "A man raises a goose within a narrow-mouthed bottle. Now that the goose has become large, how does the man get the goose safely out of the bottle without hurting the goose or damaging the bottle?"

The master says he will revisit the rich man every 24 hours until the riddle is answered, at a charge of one million dollars a day.

At the end of the first day, the rich man is troubled. He is no closer to the answer and now owes the Zen master a million dollars. When the master returns on day two and three, the rich man is more and more upset, unable to solve the riddle, with the debt clock ticking away at one million dollars per diem.

On day four, when the master returns, the rich man is jubilant. He says he has solved the riddle. "Ain't my goose," he says, "Ain't my bottle." That is, the unanswerable question is not really his problem. It is an artificial construct of no particular importance to him other than the burden and cost that he voluntarily assigned to it. Happily he walks out the door, leaving behind an unanswerable riddle that he has recognized is of no real significance, a barrier to his happiness only if he allows it to be. Presumably he will find more contentment in the future by identifying which unsolvable problems that demoralize him need not be his burden.

In the more ancient and enigmatic version of the story, the Zen master Nansen poses the riddle to a public official. Again, there is no possible rational solution and the official is stumped. Nansen claps his hands, shouts the official's name, and declares, "Now the goose is out!" End of story.

Since there is no particular right answer, I will state my own theory. Perhaps in this story, the bottle represents our own imaginary constraints. We are the goose! We have grown up in that bottle, not even realizing that there exists a life outside the artificial restrictions that seem so real to us. By recognizing the illusory nature of the bottle, with a clap of the hands we are free.

Think about whether each bottle that constrains you is real.

Burning Bushes

We are all philosophers. We map out the storyline for our life, and daily enact creative scenes as new characters are introduced and new situations arise. It is up to us to decide where meaning is to be found, a very exciting opportunity.

Yet, for those who do not actively choose the philosophical principles that will guide them, a default position exists. It is the artificial system of their culture, the system most of their peers accept and thereby reinforce. Most people in any culture accept the default position, treating that set of assumptions as if they possess independent validity.

I personally realized in my 30s that many of our culture's interwoven unwritten rules were arbitrary, and I chose to seek my own path. I had a meaningful job as a doctor, but for some 10 years I could not find a deeper story line that would add a greater context to my life. I eventually put aside my philosophical search and watched the events of my life play out without a theme to hold them together. I was happily married, my life was fine, and I had come to the conclusion that life events could be accepted as independent chapters without a unifying story.

In one of those quirky and improbable events that might have had no effect on my life but instead changed everything, another doctor invited me to lunch. I was now in my mid-40s, and had given up my philosophical quest a decade before. I had been considering from time to time how one might know if Divinity really existed. If the Bible or essentially any other religious holy text were true, miracles commonly happened in those ancient days, but I had never been aware of a single one in my own life. I would welcome a miracle just as much as the Biblical figures did. Was the Bible false in reporting so many divine miracles, or had the world changed since then?

This question had occupied me for a couple of years. I wanted a miracle. Just one. I planned to be broad-minded and accept any miracle, though I did have a personal favorite if I could order one a la carte. Recall the Biblical tale of God summoning Moses through a burning bush after Moses had been banished from Egypt for striking a guard. Speaking to Moses through the legendary bush that was bathed in flames but not consumed by the fire, God ordered him back to Egypt to free the Hebrew slaves. Moses recognized the supernatural power behind this spectacle because it defied the laws of nature and was a one-of-a-kind occurrence. After all, if such a bush were commonplace, it would merely appear ordinary, just another bush. Would you still consider a bush that burned without being consumed miraculous if every house had one? Yet the very miracle that I hoped for but never expected to find was a burning bush through which I, like Moses in the Biblical story, received divine guidance.

And so the matter rested for several years, as a quiet and vague thought at the back of my mind that I considered only rarely. Over that time, I did not see a single recognizable miracle. The problem seemed to me to be on the supply side - I didn't see any miracles because there weren't any. So now I was sitting alone in a doctor's waiting room as he finished his morning schedule, before we would go to lunch together. The doctor had only one magazine in his waiting room, a scientific one giving brief life histories of famous scientists. I picked it up without enthusiasm and opened it randomly.

I had opened the magazine to an article about the French scientist Antoine Laurent Lavoisier, who lived in the 1700s and died via the guillotine in the French Revolution. It seems that in addition to his scientific pursuits, Lavoisier was a leader of the King's tax collection program, which did not make him a popular figure with the peasants when they revolted (hence, the guillotine). The article noted that Lavoisier was credited with discovering that the process of respiration, which takes place in the cells of our body, is the same process as the combustion that burns the wood in our fireplace or creates a candle flame. In our cells and in our body as a whole, oxygen we inhale from the atmosphere is combined with nutrients from the food we eat to fuel our metabolism and keep us burning at approximately 98.6 degrees. The process, in addition to consuming oxygen and generating heat, gives off water and carbon dioxide (which we exhale), essentially the same chemistry as occurs in a burning fireplace log.

As I read this, a thought began stirring within me. It wasn't exactly a lightning bolt; one brain neuron seemed to be slowly prodding another over the course of a few days. Gradually, an idea grew. Though the wood and the candle are consumed by their fire, we are not. Partly this is because our internal fire is tightly controlled metabolically so that we don't ignite into a blaze, and partly it is because we keep replenishing the fuel as well as our body's infrastructure with fresh nutrients each time we eat. This fire of life persists until our death, but is transmitted from generation to generation, just as one candle can light another in an endless chain. From the first time the spark of life entered our world, this flame has been transmitted through the eons to us. Molecules that happened to be passing through our mothers at the time of our gestation were arranged in orderly fashion and then ignited with the flame of life. *Incredibly, I had found my burning bush, and it was me!*

The miracle I sought had not been hidden at all - it was Me! I had been looking for the rare unduplicated event as a sign of a miracle, while viewing my own life as routine. Suddenly I realized that I myself was the bush that burned without being consumed, and so are you. All animal life IS the process of burning without being consumed. I was a burning bush in a world filled with burning bushes, miracles disguised by being commonplace, hidden from me only by my own blindness.

The months that followed were the most intellectually exciting of my life. I began looking at the objects around me and thinking about the story each had to tell.

Suddenly I not only had a spiritual breakthrough, but a Rosetta stone for interpreting the world in a different way. Miracles were everywhere, disguised by their commonness, and I had indeed been tripping over them all my life. Flashing into sharp focus was a planet in which living organisms were formed from the atoms of rock and dirt. I looked with new eyes at trees, grass, clouds, and stars. Any conversation, any relationship became to me an interchange between miraculous beings. The old fight for success, for achievement, the daily battle of man against the world, had dissolved for me once I began unwrapping this magnificent treasure I had already been given.

My career as a doctor was immediately transformed. I realized that since life is a miracle, each of my patients was as miraculous as I. My job was to take care of the amazing individual across the desk from me - what a glorious opportunity I had!

Together we burn with life.

We might think of a campfire as being the same entity at 10 p.m. that it was at 7 p.m., though we realize we have tossed new logs on the fire all evening to sustain it, and the campfire is composed of different logs over the course of time. What about ourselves? Since birth, the chemicals of our body are continually replaced and exchanged with the outside world; we add atoms meal by meal and exchange atoms breath by breath. Guy Murchie, Chicago Tribune reporter, photographer, and author, in *The Seven*

Mysteries of Life points out that even the DNA that encodes the genetic master plan is likewise continually exchanging its atoms with the environment. [9] We are not then a closed set of chemicals but rather a dynamic process of open exchange in which a constantly varying collection of atoms is brought to life by this fire by which we burn but are not consumed. We share the world with other living things likewise carrying and transmitting the flame lit long ago by the same unknowable torch. This world, in which cars and air conditioners break down at the most inconvenient times, is above all a most remarkable place.

Every person, every animal that you see burns without being consumed. Your body is a process that collects fuel with each meal, distributes it to every cell via blood vessels, and inhales oxygen from the atmosphere to perpetuate the cellular fire. Internal chemicals such as enzymes regulate the combustion to an optimal temperature. You are the oven, you are the fuel, you are the fire.

How amazing you are! And every person you see is equally amazing. Every bird that flies, every squirrel in the tree, is a controlled flame just like you. Look at any animal as the fire that is its nature, the fire that burns but does not consume. Surely you are a miracle in a world of miracles.

The Blank Page

In *Nine Gates to the Chassidic Mysteries*, Jiri Langer, a Hebrew and Czech poet, scholar, and teacher, described his life in Chassidic Eastern Europe in an impoverished Jewish community of the early 20th century. In describing life within his community, Langer writes about the sanctity of holy texts. He points out that the holiest Jewish text is the Torah, composed of the first five books of the Bible, written in Hebrew. While every letter is sacred, most sacred of all is the blank page on which the letters are written. [10]

However, in this life with our human limitations, we lack the ability to understand the blank page, which represents ultimate truth. The best we can manage is to try to understand the letters on the page, aware of their limits. Writing only captures the tangible, the finite, and will never capture the infinite. Words all carry a point of view; words lead to rules and interpretations, while Infinity slips through the spaces between the letters.

Langer's problem was not confined to his era. On our own spiritual quest, we must negotiate paths already paved with words and rules, while we seek the blank page of Infinity and Eternity. Sometimes for a moment, the words disappear, and we are left face to face with the blank page. This moment can be frightening or blissful or both, the wordless encounter with that for which there are no words.

Without words, such experiences cannot be transmitted, but they strike a chord deep inside that cannot be forgotten. Paraphrasing Pulitzer Prize-winning author Annie Dillard, we become aware that all along we have been an instrument capable of playing this very chord, but never knew it before. [11] Such moments may come randomly, and only to those whose hearts are open and accepting. But even one such encounter is enough to change a life forever. One moment you are caught up in all the plots and counterplots of mundane life, and then suddenly you sense the blank page beyond all words, and feel the Infinite expressing itself in you. Part of being human is the possibility of recognizing at any moment that you are an instrument played by Eternity. We don't need to view the miraculous from a distance; we merely need to contemplate the true nature of ourselves. The Infinite is as close as your next breath.

Suspended Between Tigers

There is an old Eastern allegory in which a man is chased to the edge of a cliff by a hungry tiger. With no other means of escape, the man climbs down a vine hanging over the edge of the cliff, where he momentarily finds safety out of reach of his pursuer. Alas, from below comes another roar, this one from yet another tiger on a lower ridge but also out of reach of the man, still clinging for his life to the vine. There hangs the man, suspended between two tigers.

Sometimes it is best in an allegory not to get emotionally attached to the characters. The man becomes aware that his weight is beginning to tug the vine's roots loose, and it will soon pull out of the ground. At about this time, the man realizes his temporary lifeline is a grapevine, on which ripe grapes dangle. Before the vine can detach and fall, the man grasps one of the grapes, puts it into his mouth, and swallows it.

Sizing up his situation, he says, "This grape is delicious!"

And here you and I stand now, suspended between tigers, the tigers that chased us and the tigers that await us. If we focus on the tigers, which is the response of most of us, we feel great stress. It is certainly a world with plenty of metaphorical tigers; they pursued us in the past and will do so in the future.

The key to happiness is to focus in this instant on the grape. Perhaps the grape tastes even sweeter, knowing as we do that our world contains tigers, and we cannot banish all of them. Our happiness is dependent on recognizing the sweetness of life's experiences as they occur, without letting our awareness of past and future tigers overshadow the moment. Can you appreciate that the grapes are delicious, suspended as we are between tigers?

THE MIRACLE OF EARTH

The world is a mystery. This, what you're looking at, is not all there is to it.

Carlos Castaneda
Journey to Ixtlan

Not only is the Universe stranger than we think, it is stranger than we can think.

Werner Heisenberg
Across the Frontiers

To make an apple pie from scratch, you must first create the universe.

Carl Sagan

Fish on a Bridge

Many years ago, my family and I went camping on a December weekend. I noted that the thermometer reading was 30 degrees. I awoke much earlier than 8 a.m. to find fog over the lake, and was fascinated all morning by the varying patterns of sun and fog. Numerous times throughout the morning I walked onto a fishing bridge for a vantage point to observe this mysterious interplay. Over the course of at least two hours, I kept stepping around a dead five-inch fish lying on the bridge. On one such trip, one of my children saw the fish move. I looked, and the apparently dead fish had begun flipping around. I nudged the fish off the bridge into the water and watched it gracefully swim away.

Where did the fish come from? How long had it been there? All night? Certainly for at least two hours. What had I just seen? I have spoken with several people who pointed out that the fish was probably cold enough to be in a state of suspended animation until the morning's relative warmth stirred its metabolism back to an active state. I likewise found within myself a strong bias to presume a natural explanation. Maybe the fish jumped on the bridge; maybe it was dropped and forgotten by a fisherman (though we had not seen a fisherman on the lake that morning). Then surely the cold produced the dead appearance, and the sun brought the apparent miracle.

And yet, how would I know a miracle if I saw one? Is a fish surviving for hours out of water simply routine? Friends told me several similar stories of prolonged fish survival out of water, and therefore were not very impressed with my story. But what if it was miraculous to those whose minds are open to miracles? How many miracles might I have missed because I felt a scientific explanation reduced an event to the ranks of the ordinary? Can I be sure there is a scientific explanation for my fish story, or are we occasionally given glimpses that a deeper realm of mystery sometimes touches our everyday experience? For that matter, if this was a divine revelation, was it for me or the fish? (I can picture that fish back in the water now, trying to get its fellow fish to believe its story).

Was I shown at least a touch of magic that morning? Do we all tend to shrink the magical to the ordinary, and then wonder why our lives lack magic? And if a fish surviving out of water is remarkable, where it can only lie still or flop around, how much more spectacular is a fish living naturally in water, with a mode of survival that has persisted for millions of years?

One, a Few, or an Infinite Number

In the 48th and final lecture of his excellent video course, *How the Earth Works*, Washington University in St. Louis geophysics professor Michael E. Wysession, Ph.D. explores the possibility that intelligent life exists elsewhere in the universe. Dr. Wysession recognizes that the question remains unanswerable, but in doing so, traces the improbable set of circumstances that allowed the development of intelligent life on Earth.

Dr. Wysession begins with the question raised in 1950 by physicist Enrico Fermi - if intelligent life is widespread in our galaxy, why have we not been contacted? Perhaps other civilizations have been unable to reach us, or are intentionally avoiding us. Perhaps civilizations self-destruct by the time they gain the technology for interstellar space travel. Or perhaps Earth is unique.

It has been stated that if the fundamental forces of nature such as gravity or electromagnetism were slightly different, the structures of our universe could not exist. Whether they are perfectly set by a Planner, occur through random chance, or exist in response to some deeper unknown principle remains beyond the realm of science.

Even in the presence of such fortuitous natural laws, Earth has led a charmed existence. Its location in the Milky Way Galaxy has been ideal, situated somewhat peripherally on one of the arms of the spiral galaxy. Most stars in a galaxy are located more centrally, where the many nearby stars emit intense radiation, hurl bombardments of comets, and erupt in frequent supernovas that prevent the development of life. On planets orbiting stars farther from the center of the Milky Way than our own solar system, a dearth of elements such as metals would likewise hinder the possibility of life. Dr. Wysession estimates that only 5-10% of stars within our galaxy are in the fortunate range that could spawn living organisms.

Closer to home, a key ingredient for developing life has been the presence of liquid water on or near the planetary surface for some four billion years. Earth is the right distance from the sun to allow the existence of water-based life such as our own, and its orbit, though elliptical, is close enough to a circle to avoid traveling too close or too far from the sun to extinguish life. There have been many ice ages, many eras in which large areas of the oceans have frozen, but somehow planetary processes such as volcanic eruptions have re-thawed the Earth. Dr. Wysession states that the habitable zone around our sun only extends from 5% closer to the sun than our current orbit to about 15% farther away.

The sun itself is of a fortuitous size. Larger stars burn up more quickly and don't permit the billions of years of stability Earth has enjoyed. The habitable zone for planets orbiting smaller stars places the planets dangerously close to lethal vagaries such as solar flares.

Professor Wysession refers to the massive planet Jupiter as a good shepherd for the Earth, reducing by a factor of 10,000 the number of comets and asteroids that might otherwise bombard our planet. Even the presence of our Moon gives a gyroscope-like stabilization to our orbit. Our planet spins at a rapid enough rate to allow daytime heating and nighttime cooling to be modest, without huge swings. The tilt of Earth gives us seasons, creating a larger variety of ecological niches that stimulate evolutionary diversity.

Earth is large enough to gravitationally hold an atmosphere, but not so large that lethal gases such as hydrogen and helium are held in deadly quantities. It has a magnetic field and an ozone layer to deflect and shield us from dangerous ionizing radiation. The planet has enough radioactive isotopes deep within it to contribute warmth and to continually stir the planetary surface and interior, keeping it geologically active. It is rich with water and the kind of metals and minerals from which living organisms can form. Dr.

Wysession summarizes: "In short, Earth seems to be just the right size, just the right distance from just the right kind of star, and just the right distance from the center of the right kind of galaxy." [12]

Dr. Wysession hypothesizes that the development of life in its simplest form can likely happen on any planet with sustained liquid water on its surface. However, as a home to complex life forms, Earth might be a solitary outpost, a great rarity despite the immense number of stars and planets.

Whether there are other planets whose atoms form living organisms is currently unknowable. Yet, a look outside my window or into my mirror confirms the abundant fertility of Earth, and the existence of water-based collections of chemicals such as ourselves that have attained consciousness. To see the miracle, we need only open our eyes.

Scavenger Hunt

Your life is the result of two extremely successful scavenger hunts in which a host of exotic items were collected from around the universe and assembled. First, Earth had to collect the elements necessary for life, and then living bodies like ours had to obtain those elements from the Earth. This task was made more formidable because many items on the list did not even exist in the early universe and hence required assembly.

The universe is estimated to be about 13.7 billion years old, while our solar system - containing the sun and its planets, including Earth - is thought to have formed about 4.6 billion years ago. Most of the history of the universe occurred before there was an Earth. Key elements of living organisms, such as the oxygen that we breathe and the calcium in our bones, did not exist in the hydrogen and helium gas clouds of the early universe. By processes I'll soon describe, it took billions of years for the creation of elements that now take life within us. We are most fortunate that Earth collected these elements and packaged them into living organisms.

For example, the planet needed to accumulate oxygen in its gas form, which did not exist at the beginning of the universe and was almost totally absent from the early atmosphere of Earth. Thus some time and patience has been required. Water also needed to be procured, which was complicated by the fact that it boiled away at the high temperatures of the early Earth. Therefore, filling up the oceans required some unique water-delivery mechanisms after the Earth had cooled a bit.

Then came the task of gathering a host of elements, some of them rare, and making living bodies out of them. Most of the atoms of the known universe are hydrogen, a key component of the water on which earthly life is based, and almost all the rest are inert helium, which bodies do not use. Only about 2% of the universe's atoms are not hydrogen or helium, and your body makes spectacular use of them. Of that special 2% that are not hydrogen or helium, the commonest of the remaining atoms are oxygen, carbon, and nitrogen, which are fundamental in building earthly bodies. About 99% of your body is made of six elements - oxygen, carbon, hydrogen, nitrogen, calcium, and phosphorus - but several dozen other elements, some of great importance, make up the other 1%. Biomedical scientist Anne Marie Helmenstine, Ph.D. estimates, in an Internet posting, that the elements of your body, if sold as chemicals, would be worth about one American dollar. [13] This doesn't seem like a lucrative payoff for scouring the universe to collect all these elements, but their value is enhanced when they are assimilated into a body and brought to life. A preliminary step in this tricky process requires macerating and pulverizing the Earth's surface rock into a thin layer of soil and assembling living bodies out of the soil.

Presently it is the extremely talented molecule deoxyribonucleic acid, better known as DNA, that lines up the atoms in living bodies, and choreographs their dance, though other molecules such as ribonucleic acid (RNA) likely played that role in the past. It is also through its DNA that each organism reproduces, providing instructions for turning planetary dirt and air into current and future organisms. No one knows where the first DNA came from, though it is very proficient at replicating itself through the living organisms it generates. It has even been said that bodies are the way DNA generates more DNA. Precursor molecules with similarities to DNA subunits have been found on asteroids and comets, so it is possible these rocky visitors from space may have crash-landed onto the early Earth with ingredients from which DNA and RNA could be formed.

Let us examine some of the items on your scavenger hunt list, and explore how you came to acquire them. As part of your body, these elements are indeed quite precious, so you will want to take good care of your collection.

Inhaling the Atmosphere

Fish do it. So do lizards. So do we. Although these introductory words could apply to many commonalities we share with other life forms, I'm referring to breathing. All organisms must find a way to maintain their internal environment while immersed in their external environment, and breathing is part of that interchange. There is certainly no such thing as independent living when every terrestrial plant requires a continual intake of carbon dioxide from the air, and every animal's survival requires a continuous external supply of oxygen. Your independent existence lasts only until your next breath.

Every organism has the ability to take from the outside world the elements it needs for survival and to discharge back into the outside world the wastes that would otherwise turn the organism into a garbage dump. These skills must be present at the moment of birth, innate.

Animal life on Earth is dependent on the intake of oxygen to react with internally stored fuel sources such as carbohydrates, proteins, and fats to produce the energy that sustains us. We typically have enough stored fuel to survive for weeks until we absolutely must have food or perish, but we could not survive for more than a few minutes without oxygen. That oxygen now constitutes 20.95% of our atmosphere, and dissolved oxygen from the atmosphere makes its way into bodies of water to sustain fish and other gill-breathing aquatic life.

Earth's primordial atmosphere was almost entirely carbon dioxide (CO_2) with hardly any molecular oxygen in a form we could breathe, so we could not have survived in that era. Should someone in your neighborhood invent a time machine and offer you a trip back to those early days of Earth, you would be wise to politely decline. In addition to the fiery climate and pesky meteor bombardments, the absence of oxygen would have been a killer. The first organisms that tapped sunlight as an energy source originated the process of photosynthesis, which consumes carbon dioxide and gives off oxygen. These one-celled organisms, called cyanobacteria, and the various hierarchies of plants that subsequently developed, released into the atmosphere the oxygen that was a waste product of photosynthesis.

Only after microorganisms and plants had modified the atmosphere by discharging oxygen into it could animals survive. Hence the oxygen atoms we breathe now were previously part of plants that processed and released these atoms into the air - who knows how many living organisms previously held the oxygen atoms in our next breath?

We live imbedded in air and interpenetrated by it. Canadian environmentalist and zoologist, David Suzuki, Ph.D. in *The Sacred Balance* describes the interface between our lungs and the air we draw into them: "The line where air leaves off and our cells begin is blurred. Categories merge here - gaseous and liquid, outside and inside - as the planet's atmosphere enters our bloodstream." [14]

Where the atmosphere meets the air pockets in our lungs, called alveoli, atmospheric oxygen is drawn across biological membranes into our blood, where it attaches to the hemoglobin molecules in red blood cells. These serve as couriers to deliver the oxygen to all the cells of our body. Within our lungs, the branched structures of our airways offer a huge surface area for air exchange, similar to the area of a tennis court, neatly packed inside our chest. [15] Oxygen atoms that before our most recent breath were outside of us are now being carried to all the cells of our body to fuel the metabolic processes that we call life. Suzuki writes, "So air always remains within us and is as much a part of our bodies as any tissue or organ. We are a part of the air, which in turn is a part of all green plants and every other breathing creature." [16]

In the process of human metabolism (and all animal metabolism), carbon dioxide is generated, which is then carried by the blood back to the lungs, where it is exhaled into the atmosphere. The carbon dioxide does not usually stay free in the atmosphere for long, because plants quickly draw it into their own bodies, keeping the atmospheric concentration of carbon dioxide well below one percent (currently about .035%).

Suzuki provides a couple of thought experiments to envision the interpenetration of organism and atmosphere. Imagine a number of people sharing a room - perhaps in a restaurant - breathing. After outlining the mathematics, Suzuki concludes, "Even the crudest calculation reveals that each of us very quickly absorbs atoms into our bodies that were once an integral part of everyone else in the room, and vice versa." [17] In fact, via breathing, we continually interchange atoms with our co-workers, clients, neighbors, pets, and houseplants, as well as millions upon millions of people, plants, and animals we will never encounter.

Suzuki cites the thought experiment of Harvard astronomer Harlow Shapley dealing with argon gas, which is an inert (non-reacting) gas making up about one percent of the atmosphere. After performing calculations regarding how many argon atoms we would take in with each breath and how many breaths we take, certain non-intuitive conclusions follow. "All people over the age of 20 have taken at least 100 million breaths and have inhaled argon atoms that were emitted in the first breath of every child born in the world a year before!" [18]

Suzuki quotes Shapley, "Your next breath will contain more than 400,000 of the argon atoms that Ghandi [sic] breathed in his long life. Argon atoms are here from the conversations at the Last Supper, from the arguments of diplomats at Yalta, and from the recitations of the classic poets. We have argon from the sighs and pledges of ancient lovers, from the battle cries at Waterloo... " [19]

Although we can exercise conscious control over our breathing, the act is generally an automatic function regulated by ancient mechanisms within the brainstem. All living things on Earth share the same atmosphere, which crosses man-made borders and links all forms of life. We must treat the air with respect, knowing that what we put into the atmosphere will soon be within us.

In the words of Suzuki: "Every breath is a sacrament, an essential ritual. As we imbibe this sacred element, we are physically linked to all of our present biological relatives, countless generations that have preceded us and those that will follow." [20] No act is more critical to you than your next breath. Recognize that act as the miracle that it is.

Breathing Stardust

Before you take any more breaths into your body, you might want to make inquiries about where that oxygen has been. After all, oxygen is powerful stuff; it is the stuff that allows fires to burn and metals to rust. If our atmospheric oxygen level were much higher than its current 21%, fires could become uncontrollable with the slightest spark, and rust unstoppable. If oxygen levels were much lower, we would not be here to tell the story.

Oxygen was not a charter member of the universe, which according to the Big Bang Theory began with a burst of pure energy. Part of this energy condensed into the gas clouds of space, mostly hydrogen and a much smaller amount of helium. Most stars even today are primarily made of those ingredients. If your high school chemistry teacher gave you such a mixture of hydrogen and helium gas and challenged you to make some little moons and planets with it, you would run into technical difficulties. For one thing, both gases are lighter than air and would tend to float toward the upper atmosphere and escape the Earth. For another, helium under terrestrial conditions is essentially chemically inert and would not react with other substances. These ingredients do not seem to provide a very promising recipe for creating the vast multiplicity of forms that make up our world. Yet an entire universe of primarily hydrogen, with an admixture of helium, congealed into fiery stars, galaxies, moons, oak trees, and gerbils. We ourselves are made from transformations of that same original brew.

The universe's original hydrogen-helium gas mixture clumped gravitationally into stars, which under the influence of their own gravity continued to clump, in the process fusing hydrogen into helium while generating heat and light. These first stars and the early universe that surrounded them did not contain oxygen. When that first generation of stars fused so much hydrogen into helium that they ran below a necessary threshold amount of hydrogen, the stars underwent terminal explosions of various kinds that created unimaginable heat, synthesizing from those stellar remnants a number of new elements, including oxygen. Thus, this leading character in the drama of our planet - oxygen - did not make its first appearance in Act One of the story of the universe when the only atoms on stage were hydrogen and helium, but it appeared long before the origin of our own solar system about 4.6 billion years ago.

Second-generation stars forming out of the universe's gas clouds included oxygen from earlier stellar explosions. Later generations of stars that ended explosively further enriched interstellar space's gaseous mixture with still more oxygen. It is uncertain how many stars in their demise contributed oxygen to the gas clouds that condensed into our Sun, our solar system, and ultimately into us.

Guy Murchie reported that oxygen constitutes only one-eighteenth of one percent of the atoms in the known universe. [21] Yet Earth is a veritable hotbed of oxygen. Since our bodies are constructed from the chemicals of Earth and its atmosphere, and since almost all life on Earth is water based, oxygen becomes an even bigger player. More than half of our body is water, which contains two molecules of hydrogen and one of oxygen, the same ratio that fills our oceans. The atmosphere, as mentioned, is about 21% oxygen. By mass, oxygen constitutes 46.6% of the Earth and 65% of the human body. 24% of the atoms in our body are oxygen.

This amazing element, synthesized during the death throes of ancient stars, after drifting through interstellar space where it makes up one-eighteenth of a percent of the universe, coalesced as a key puzzle piece with which our solar system, our planet, and our bodies were constructed. It has the power to support the combustion within our cells of elements from the pizza we ate yesterday, giving us a temperature of about 98.6 degrees, and in doing so, giving us life. Your body is a furnace that oxygen has brought to life. Your dog, your cat, the armadillo in the back yard, and the butterfly are other models of furnaces in which oxygen, after an interstellar odyssey lasting millions or billions of years, sustains life here and now, at this very moment.

There are all sorts of chemical processes within the Earth that bind or release oxygen. It cycles between planet and atmosphere and living organisms over and over. There really isn't any way to track all the places where the oxygen that you will inhale with your next breath has been or where it will go after you recycle it back into circulation. But it will be there for your next breath and the ones that follow. Oxygen's cosmic journey intersects with and perpetuates our own personal journey on the third planet from our Sun.

Water (Drinking the Oceans)

You probably don't give much thought to the process of drinking a glass of water. Yet here sits lifeless water in the glass at one moment, and a few swallows later, it is a critical part of your living body. In fact, water is by far the biggest molecular component of your body, averaging about 60% of you by weight. Babies are about three-fourths water, and we slowly but steadily get drier as we age, till we are about half water in old age.

Life on Earth is water-based, and the persistence of earthly life has been dependent on the presence of surface water on our planet for some four billion years. Wrap a membrane around water, enclose just the right elements within the membrane (there's the difficult part!), and you have the possibility of a living

46

cell. Combine single living cells to form multicellular bodies and you have water-filled, water-dependent organisms.

Water consists of two atoms of hydrogen bound to one of oxygen. It is probably no fluke that water is such an essential component of our world and us. There are far more hydrogen atoms in the universe than all other atoms added together. Hydrogen is also the oldest element. The hydrogen atoms in our bodies today are estimated to be over 13 billion years old, remnants from the dawn of the universe. Although hydrogen is also the lightest element, it provides about 63% of the atoms that make up each of us, but only 10% of our weight. Thus the water on which earthly life is based is a union between hydrogen, the universe's oldest and commonest element, and oxygen, formed in terminal stellar explosions. This mix of ancient intergalactic atoms is the stuff you bathe in, water the plants with, and drink to sustain your existence.

The hydrogen atoms of water have been described as attaching to the oxygen like a pair of Mickey Mouse ears, so that the hydrogen atoms tend to be on one side of the water molecule and the oxygen on the other, an arrangement called dipolar. This allows many of the special properties that make water truly the elixir of life.

For example, water has been called a universal solvent. While this is something of an overstatement, water has a remarkable power to dissolve and hold chemicals within it. Many of the key metabolic reactions within living organisms can only happen between chemicals that have been dissolved. That is why you water your lawn after fertilizing it, to dissolve the components within the fertilizer so that they can be soaked into the soil and absorbed through roots in the dissolved form necessary to perform life-enhancing biochemical reactions in the plants.

You yourself must likewise maintain a sufficient water intake to keep the elements of your body at optimal concentrations for the metabolic processes of life. In my years as a doctor, I was constantly amazed at how effortlessly we accomplish this. Small changes in water concentration cause the posterior pituitary gland to raise or lower its production of anti-diuretic hormone (ADH), which serves as a messenger ordering the kidneys to raise or lower their excretion of water. Receptors within our vascular system and dryness within our mouth notify appropriate brain centers when we need to drink fluids, and we find ourselves responding to subtle signals we perceive as thirst. We are not cognizant that our sodium levels are creeping up or down - we just grab the right beverage to instinctively replenish our supplies. Our kidneys then perform the fine-tuning, adjusting water and mineral excretion to maintain a remarkably stable internal environment.

The primeval Earth was thought to have once been too hot to have surface liquid water. In fact, in *Life in the Universe*, astronomers and planetary scientists, Jeffrey Bennett, Seth Shostak, and Bruce Jakosky speculate that our water has a very exotic history. [22] Planets like Earth were built by a process called accretion, in which gravitational attraction pulls together small objects called planetesimals to form larger ones, until full-sized planets are formed. During this era, Earth was too hot for surface liquid water to exist.

The authors state, "Thus, if Earth had formed exclusively from these 'local' planetesimals, there would have been no water to form our oceans and no gases to form our atmosphere. The simplest way to account for the presence of water and gas is to assume that at least a few water-bearing planetesimals from farther out in the solar system crashed into the young Earth. This assumption makes sense, because even today our planet occasionally is hit by asteroids or comets that formed beyond Earth's orbit. We do not yet know whether most of the water and gas was brought to Earth by asteroids that formed far enough from the Sun to include at least some water or by icy comets that formed in the neighborhood of the jovian planets [Jupiter, Saturn, Uranus, and Neptune]. Either way, the water we drink and the air we breathe likely were once part of objects orbiting beyond the orbit of Mars." [23]

The water and gas from these extraterrestrial asteroids and comets became part of Earth as it gradually began to cool. Such materials would initially just be part of the mix of the planet. Through volcanic eruptions, material from within the Earth was hurled into the newly forming atmosphere, a process called outgassing. To quote Bennett et al, "Outgassing probably released most of the water vapor that condensed to form our oceans as well as most of the gas that formed our atmosphere." [24] By this point, Earth had cooled enough that its water did not boil away, and could begin its series of transformations on our planet.

Visitations from ice-bearing comets are now far less frequent, and our finite world has essentially a finite amount of water. 97.2% of Earth's water is the saltwater of the ocean. Of the remaining 2.8%, which primarily consists of all the world's fresh water, 2.1% is frozen in icecaps and glaciers. Approximately 0.0001% of the world's fresh water is easily accessible. [25] Problem: Terrestrial organisms such as ourselves require fresh salt-free water to survive on a planet in which 97.2% of the water is the salty variety of the oceans. Solution: Earth comes to our rescue.

Fresh water continually regenerates in what is called the "hydrologic cycle." Water leaves its salt load behind as it evaporates from the oceans, is carried invisibly hundreds or thousands of miles through the atmosphere, precipitates as freshwater rain that supports essentially all terrestrial life, and then any runoff makes its way back through streams and rivers to the ocean. After a rain, the roots of plants drink the water from the soil. As water is evaporated from leaves, a negative pressure is created in the leaves that draws water up from the roots, through stems and trunks and branches to replenish the leaves, but this water does not travel alone. It carries with it dissolved nutrients from the soil, chemicals of Earth that are about to transform from lifeless soil atoms to the tissue of living plants. In the next step of their alchemy, plants are able to harness sunlight via photosynthesis, but can only turn that energy into life through the medium of water and the dissolved chemicals it carries.

Water serves as the means of circulation both within living organisms and on the surface of Earth. Ocean currents soak up heat from the tropics and transmit that heat toward the poles. The Atlantic Gulf Stream, for example, carries warm water from near the equator and routes it northward to warm the climate of Europe. Oceans seasonally and daily store heat during warm weather and release it during cool weather, moderating climate. Rivers carry not only water, but also the chemicals of the rock through which they travel, and transmit their load to the oceans. Hence, oceans are salty due to the accumulation over eons of salts transmitted by the rivers of the world and discharged into the sea.

70.8% of the Earth's surface is ocean, and life is presumed to have begun there. The ocean never experiences a drought, and has been steadily inhabitable at least somewhere for some 4 billion years. Yet surprisingly, Professor Michael Wysession points out that only about one-fifth of one percent of the world's biomass lives in the ocean. [26] Ecosystems are built on plant life at the base of their food chains, and it isn't easy being an ocean plant. Terrestrial plants have exposure to sunlight and ready access to photosynthesis. Only the very top of oceans gets enough sunlight to serve this purpose. When terrestrial plants need nutrients from the Earth, they extract them with roots that reach into the dirt of the planet. Any plants that might consider living on the surface of an ocean would find it difficult to send roots several miles down to the seafloor. Therefore, only coastal waters and shallow sea shelves near land have enough sunlight to reach plants rooted at the bottom, and therefore the greatest concentration of sea life is in shallow waters. There are fertile oceanic ecosystems where the upwelling of sediments from the ocean bottom supplies nutrients for expansive communities of fish close to the surface. These areas are more likely to be located near land rather than in the vast expanses of the deep blue seas.

Along the surface of oceans, where exposure to sunlight makes photosynthesis possible, floating algae and plankton are the main photosynthesizers. In fact, much of the photosynthesis in the whole world is performed by these tiny organisms floating at the tops of oceans, which are then eaten by a succession of smaller fish that get eaten by bigger fish. Nonetheless, well over 99% of the biomass on the planet is terrestrial, dependent on that most precious fresh water that evaporates from the oceans. All the life that you see represents transformations of water into living form.

To quote Suzuki: "Water enters our bodies, circulates through it to the rhythm of the heart, ceaselessly carrying food, fuel, and cellular and molecular detritus to and from various organs of the body. Water seeps through our skin and escapes from our lungs as vapour and exits every opening of the body. It then reenters the hydrological cycle, trickling into the soil, entering plants, evaporating into the atmosphere, entering bodies of water. In this way, water circulates endlessly from the heavens to the oceans and land, held briefly within all living things before continuing the cycle." [27]

We ourselves daily recycle about 3% of the water in our body, restocking with a trip to the water fountain or a glass of orange juice. Each molecule of water has its own long history, perhaps including drifting for millions of years as ice on a comet in the far reaches of our solar system before finding its way to the glass of fruit juice that is about to take life within you.

The novelist and poet Jorge Luis Borges was speaking of water when he said:

Your flights are called the Euphrates or the Ganges.

(They claim it is holy, the water of the latter,
but, as the seas work in their secret ways
and the planet is porous, it may still be true
to claim all men have bathed in the Ganges.)

"Poem of the Fourth Element" [28]

Having a drink of water, like taking a breath, is a miraculous and holy act. When you drink your next glass of water, think about the amazing sacrament you are performing.

Tale of the Living Dirt

Deep inside the Earth, radioactive isotopes churn the interior of the planet, roiling up rock flows that slide the continents around. Those continents drift under an atmosphere of windswept gases. At the interface where the turbulent interior of the planet and its swirling atmosphere come together, we live out our lives walking the planet's surface, with its deceptive appearance of calm stability.

The surface we walk upon we call soil or dirt. It is from this thin layer that the bodies of terrestrial organisms such as ourselves are made. In his book *Dirt*, arborist and "Quill & Trowel" award-winning author William Bryant Logan asks, "How can I stand on the ground every day and not feel its power? How can I live my life stepping on this stuff and not wonder at it?" [29]

Wind and rain, ice and thaw, the flow of chemicals, the assault of acids - the grinding changes of season upon season - may take centuries to generate a single centimeter of soil from the Earth's bedrock. The glaciers of multiple ice ages acted like giant plows, fragmenting rock into the tiny particles that now serve as rich farmland on multiple continents (including our own). Eons of organisms formed their bodies from the chemicals of this soil, and in their death, added their own molecules back to the mixture to be utilized again and again by subsequent generations of Earth's species. It is a basic truth that all living things are eventually recycled, and as Logan points out, "Dirt is the gift of each to all." [30]

Terrestrial plants live by capturing the energy of sunlight to synthesize their bodies and ultimately reproduce. Plants selectively extract from dirt the elements necessary for their survival, and animals with their hungers and thirsts construct their own bodies by passing the plants' energy and atoms down the food chain. You or a geranium do not need to calculate how much carbon or magnesium must be acquired; bodies have an internal genius for self-synthesis.

Plants need carbon, which they primarily "breathe in" from the air as carbon dioxide, similar to the dependence of animals on atmospheric oxygen. A plant's other key chemicals are primarily drawn in through their roots from the upper layer of soil and eventually given back to the soil after the plant's death. Humus is the name given to the upper layer of soil, stocked with organic nutrients from the recycling of prior living things, perforated by air pockets and the tunnels of earthworms, recipient of rainwater. In the words of Logan, "Humus itself is a dynamic creature, comprising a fast-changing part that liberates nitrogen and micronutrients for direct absorption by plant roots, a slow-changing, stable part that holds water, and a porous material that is easy for roots to penetrate." [31]

The rock from which soil is made is the rock of continents, which floats on the surface of the Earth supported by the denser material deep within the planet. Different locations on Earth's surface have chemically different bedrock, resulting in chemically different soil when that bedrock is ground up by the weathering processes of Nature. Different soils support different ecosystems. We, and essentially all other terrestrial living things, survive on the fecundity of those fragile few feet of soil at the interface between the mighty forces within the Earth and the gases of the atmosphere as we float through the near-vacuum of space. It is at this charmed borderland between immensities that terrestrial life exists in all its abundance.

The chemicals that soil has to offer depend on its history, the characteristics of its bedrock, the winds that have borne it to this spot, the life forms through which its atoms have passed. The soil serves as the link between the non-living chemicals from which it is made and the life to which it gives birth.

If we think, not in terms of discrete things, but in terms of interactions, a truer understanding of the world emerges. A plant is not an isolated thing. It catches sunlight for energy, while probing the soil for the minerals and nutrients it needs. These chemicals must generally be dissolved to be absorbed and utilized, so water provides the vehicle for transport and transformation, the universal currency of life. As Logan says, "The processes of growth, decay, feeding, digestion, excretion, attack, and repulsion all need wetness and generate heat. To understand them, you have to study the interconnections, not the essences." [32]

The soil itself is packed with life. It has been estimated that at least as much biomass exists below the soil surface as above it. In addition to the root systems of all plants and trees, there exist legions of insects, worms, larvae, bacteria, and fungi in countless species known and unknown. There are thought to be billions of bacteria in each square yard of temperate soil, some of which engage in chemical warfare against each other. Our scientists are now busily testing many of the compounds that soil bacteria secrete, hoping to find effective anti-bacterial agents for human use.

Logan catalogs several key substances originally secreted by soil organisms that we now deploy against germs. [33] In 1943, the antibiotic streptomycin was discovered in secretions of soil bacteria. Penicillin was discovered in 1928 when Alexander Fleming observed the bacteria-killing effect of a mold he found growing on a watermelon. The family of antibiotics called cephalosporins was found secreted by bacteria living in an Italian drainage pipe in the mid-20th century. The antibiotic Erythromycin was made from Philippine soil bacteria.

These soil inhabitants, like all living organisms, engage in positive and negative interactions with other organisms, fight battles, eat and are eaten, organize planetary chemicals into living form, and then upon their death bequeath those organized chemicals back into the life-giving soil to be recycled over and over. The soil actually breathes with the collective exchange between earth and atmosphere of oxygen and carbon dioxide by the countless microscopic denizens to which the soil is the site of their birth, life, and death. Legendary to soil scientists is the heroic and lowly earthworm, which takes soil in one end and concentrates and enriches it before excreting it out the other end, meanwhile carving tunnels in the soil through which air and water can penetrate. Human gardeners are generally cheered by the presence of a healthy number of earthworms breaking up and enriching their soil.

It is true that humans receive about as much nutrition worldwide from the consumption of fish as from the consumption of land animals such as cows and chickens. However, the most common food worldwide by far is grain, so some 98% of human nutrition is dependent upon agriculture, and therefore directly dependent on the ability of soil to continually bring forth life. [34] About 12% of the land surface is now cropland and 24% is pasture, as we strive to feed a burgeoning population on a finite planet.

Essentially all the nutrition we receive comes from eating what was itself once alive. We are not the first body in which the atoms that now compose us were brought to life. These atoms have

54

likely been components of many previous organisms, and will move on to form other combinations elsewhere in the weeks, months, and years to come. Other atoms and molecules from our future meals will replace the ones we have lost, to continually remake and remodel the always-changing entity we refer to as "me."

In the developed world, depending upon the country, the average male weighs about 150-200 pounds and the average female 120-165. It has been estimated that to maintain this weight, the average person consumes up to 60 tons of food and beverages over the course of a lifetime. [35] What a transformation this represents!

It is a world of transformations. The atmosphere transforms Earth's rock into soil, whose atoms are reorganized into living beings. Living organisms in turn have further transformed our planet and atmosphere, which through their continual interplay have breathed life and consciousness into us. We are continually exchanging molecules with the Earth, borrowing from the life-giving few feet of soil at its surface. To quote David Suzuki, "Air is the breath of life, water the drink and the earth the food of life." [36]

The landscape we see around us gives us a view of planetary rock undergoing transformation. The plants that we see are what they are because of their ability to order earthly chemicals into their living shape and tap sunlight to animate their growth and reproduction. The soil, with its ability to buffer the immensities above and below it, constantly dances and exchanges its molecules with the life forms it generates. It is not just beneath us; the soil is within us.

If you are looking for more excitement and meaning in your life, you won't have to travel far. If the front page news features its usual litany of conflicts, do not allow yourself to fall victim to these narrow and pessimistic viewpoints that our media project as representative of reality.

Look at any plant or tree. Picture interstellar gases condensing into our solar system, set the timer at 4.6 billion years for preparation, add sunlight traveling 93 million miles, mix in a rain of water droplets evaporated from a distant ocean, and allow soil to serve as a womb from which a seed springs upward as an oak tree through this blend of cosmic processes. This is your Earth. Here you are, with the ability to appreciate that the place where you stand is magical.

William Bryant Logan says, "The divine is the commonest thing in the universe." [37] Step outside. Look at the ground.

Sandstorm

In *Earth: The Biography*, Iain Stewart, Scottish geologist, and John Lynch, BBC Head of History and Science, discuss the Bodele Depression, a dust-filled basin in the Sahara Desert. The authors state, "Bodele now has the dubious distinction of being the single greatest source of airborne dust on Earth." [38] It would perhaps be nice to be a world leader at something other than generating sandstorms, but this desert sand turns out to have a huge positive impact globally.

Recall that Earth's early atmosphere was primarily carbon dioxide with minimal oxygen, but later carbon dioxide breathing plants began releasing into the atmosphere the oxygen that animals such as ourselves require. At least half of the oxygen in our atmosphere is generated by tiny sea plant-like organisms called phytoplankton which are positioned near the ocean surface, taking in carbon dioxide and exhaling oxygen. Our very lives depend on this oxygen source. The phytoplankton require various minerals to live, and their survival plays a huge role in oxygenating our atmosphere. Some of the nutrients that phytoplankton need are in short supply in the middle of an ocean.

Fortunately, planetary winds sweep over the Sahara, lift up sand from the Bodele Depression, and carry it by the ton through the air. 240 million tons of Sahara sand land each year in the Atlantic Ocean, nourishing the plankton and serving as raw materials that enable the phytoplankton, via photosynthesis, to pour oxygen into the atmosphere. Recipe: Take tiny ocean organisms, add wind-blown Sahara Desert sand, and create a burst of oxygen-emitting phytoplankton. We, who so casually survive thanks to this oxygen, owe a debt of gratitude to the winds that lift sand from the Sahara.

The Sahara sand is blown thousands of miles, with some 50 million tons crossing the ocean and landing annually on the Amazon rainforest, where it acts as a sort of fertilizer. Stewart and Lynch inform us: "It has been estimated that more than half the Amazon Basin's nutrient supply comes from the Bodele Depression, a relationship that is a beautiful example of the planet operating as a complete biological system." [39]

Part of the oxygen in your most recent breath required the conveyor belt of wind delivering Sahara sand to ocean phytoplankton, whose oxygen output was further wafted along by breezes to your mouth and nose. From there it entered your body to be pumped by the heart via your bloodstream to your tissues. After this odyssey, the oxygen becomes - at least for a time - a part of you, supporting your life. Building "you" requires collecting widespread and sometimes obscure ingredients of the world, including adding desert sand to seawater and stirring with wind.

Gravity

Does it puzzle you to realize that you are stuck to this planet by an invisible process? The same gravitational force that attaches you to the ground holds the Earth in orbit around the Sun millions of miles away. Gravity is completely familiar to everyone, and fully understood by no one. A skillful basketball player who shoots more accurately than me is an intuitive physicist, calculating the necessary trajectory that will allow gravity to draw the ball through the net on its downward arc toward the center of the Earth. Somehow the various components of the universe are attracted toward each other, and the most brilliant physicist cannot explain how this happens. You can leave your sandwich on the plate to get a drink from the refrigerator, and the sandwich will still be there when you return. The drink will also remain in the glass.

Gravity played a fundamental role in making you out of the hydrogen and helium gas clouds of the early universe. It was gravity that clumped that gas into astronomical bodies, such as planets and stars, and gravity that led to the eventual inward collapse of stars that ended in their high-energy explosions, the foundry from which other natural elements like oxygen are synthesized. It was gravity that pulled together the atoms that make up Earth, including the combination of atoms that now takes life as you.

Gravity holds the atmosphere, with its 21% oxygen, in position where you can breathe it. It holds water in the Earth's low places, its oceans and lakes and rivers, allowing it to be incorporated into living organisms. Gravity draws rain down from the clouds to the planetary surface, the roots of plants, the reservoirs of cities. Earth's ecosystem is held in place by gravity.

Despite the fact that our every step is a testament to gravity, its mystery is deep. Perhaps there is an exchange of some as yet undiscovered particle between gravitationally bound objects, even millions of miles apart, and the quest for such a particle is the grail of many contemporary physicists. Albert Einstein theorized that the "stuff" of the universe contorts space, thereby creating pathways through space that cause gravitationally bound objects to be drawn toward each other. No one really understands.

Perhaps the greatest gravitational conundrum is why its value is so "perfect." It has been known since the observations of Edwin Hubble in 1929 that the universe is expanding. In an expanding universe, if gravity were too strong, the dense fireball of the early universe would have been sucked back in on itself before life could develop. If gravity were too weak, the whole thing would have been blown to smithereens in an astronomical jiffy. This is like saying that if a coin were flipped and landed on heads (gravity too strong) or tails (gravity too weak), our universe would have crash landed back into itself or scattered by now. Only with the unlikely third possibility, the coin landing on its edge, are we alive now in a suitably stable epoch of our planet's history. As Stephen Hawking, physicist and cosmologist, writes in *A Brief History of Time*, "If the rate of expansion one second after the big bang had been smaller by even one part in a hundred thousand million million, the universe would have recollapsed before it ever reached its present size." [40] Similarly, a slightly greater rate of expansion would have sent matter and energy careening outward through the frigid void before atoms could become organisms. Gravity tames expansion to that razor's edge value at which life has had time to develop and thrive.

As we survey the familiar landscape in which feet stay on the ground and soup in the bowl, we should reflect with fascination on the invisible force whose perfect value has made our life possible.

DNA

Atoms floated through the immensity of space for untold eons before being drawn together by gravity to form our planet. Then in a process beyond comprehension, those non-living chemicals came to life in bodies like ours. Most people think of the development of life from non-life as a historical event, a one-time miracle that has launched religions and baffled science. Yet our planet churns out this very miracle every moment, constantly assembling living organisms from lifeless atoms. Every day, all day long, atoms of Earth take life in the bodies of millions of species.

Somewhere on that amazing bridge between life and non-life stands the remarkable molecule DNA, which organizes lifeless atoms into living organisms. Through DNA, the rosebush makes roses and the caterpillar becomes a butterfly - now - while we look on as witnesses. If that were not miraculous enough, DNA encodes within each organism the ability to create all future generations of its species, incorporating within each the potential to turn lifeless atoms centuries in the future into more of its kind.

No one knows where, when, or how the first DNA appeared. Yet today, all organisms found on Earth contain DNA in each living cell, dictating the structure and function of every cell. The four active components of DNA are called bases; they are adenine, thymine, guanine, and cytosine, the letters that spell out all earthly life. The moment Dad's sperm penetrated Mom's egg to commingle their DNA in what is called a fertilized egg, there existed for the first time in history the precise combination of DNA that would turn earthly chemicals into you. That DNA provided the instructions to guide the multiplication of your cells,

59

transmuting planetary chemicals into the trillions of cells that now make up your body. During your gestation, your mother provided your atoms. Since birth, you have accumulated all the rest of your atoms for yourself through eating, drinking, and breathing them. Each of your cells contains the same DNA sequence of 3 billion base pairs that were found in your original fertilized egg, including approximately 20,000 genes arrayed on your 46 chromosomes (each chromosome is a long strand of DNA).

While you were still an embryo, your body began developing modules, with different sets of your 20,000 genes activated in your liver than in your heart. If you were building a house rather than a body, you would organize the work into "modules," hiring a contractor as a master planner and a bricklayer, plumber, electrician, roofer, and woodworker to be in charge of different aspects of the construction. For the module of the kitchen, the contractor might line those five other workers up each morning and give each his assignment for the day, perhaps assigning the plumber and woodworker to specific projects and telling the other three to return after lunch. For the module of the bedroom, the contractor might give assignments to the woodworker and electrician, while telling the plumber he would not be needed on that module.

Your body creates different modules by activating different genes within each module in the appropriate sequence and turning the other genes off. Think of the parallel to the way written words are formed from the same set of 26 letters in the English language. Each word is spelled by "activating" one letter at a time from the same total set of letters. The word "cat" is generated by activating "c," then "a," then "t." Other words are created from the same 26 letters, by "turning on" different letters from within the set in the proper sequence, and leaving the other letters "off." The "alphabet" of DNA consists of only four bases (as opposed to the 26 letters of the English language), but the lineup of those four bases in each of your cells consists of 3 billion bases in a row on two interwoven spirals called a double helix. All of your cells contain that same set of 3 billion bases lined up in the same order, and each of your genes is a sequence of bases within that lineup. A tree has a different sequence of DNA bases than you do, though the same four bases are involved in constructing all known organisms on Earth. Your own base sequence is unique to you, but all people are very similar in their DNA sequencing.

Thus the cells of your eyes and heart contain the same 20,000 genes, but different master genes were turned on in each of these modules, triggering different sequences of genes to be activated from within the total set, creating your magnificent eyes by activating one set of genes and your heart by activating another. Think about all the different parts of your body, all the different specialized cell types, and realize the complexity of turning on and off the right genes at the right time in the right place in all your trillions of cells.

In the human body, over 200 distinct types of cells have been identified. Each cell type represents a different combination of genes that have been activated from within the exact same 20,000-gene set that each of your cells contains. The process is not static, as every cell continually turns individual genes on and off in the appropriate sequence. Each cell's genetic processes are interwoven into networks that are part of larger networks that ultimately make up our body. During puberty, genes turn on that govern sexual development and differentiation; as we age – unfortunately - genes activate that turn joints stiff and hair gray.

Look at any scene in nature for 30 seconds. There, adapted to the environment, are a wide variety of living organisms, every individual organism containing the same DNA molecule in all of its living cells (the cells involved in sexual reproduction provide an exception to be discussed later). Those organisms you are viewing are made of specialized cells that each activate a different combination of genes from within the organism's total genome. The rose activates one set of genes in its stalk and other sets in its flowers, its leaves, and its thorns, though each cell in the plant possesses the same DNA sequence.

At present, a gene is defined as that stretch of DNA that generates one protein. That is, genes are thought to create bodies primarily by specifying where and when proteins are synthesized. Think about that for a moment - from a biochemical perspective, your wise and complicated self was apparently physically assembled by genes in different modules of your body synthesizing the right proteins in the right sequence. These proteins, consisting of long chains of amino acids, provide the main structural and functional roles in bodies. In the words of British scientist and professor Matt Ridley, "It is proteins that do almost every chemical, structural and regulatory thing that is done in the body: they generate energy, fight infection, digest food, form hair, carry oxygen and so on and on." [41]

This is not merely the way our own species generates living bodies. The presence of DNA in all life forms on Earth implies that this is a universal mechanism through which manta rays, mosquitoes, hawks, and geraniums organize the chemicals of our natural world into organisms. Within each of the specialized cells that constitute a hawk, the appropriate combination of genes turns on and off in arrays that organize atoms into wings and beak and eyes.

Of all the DNA in our cells, only about 1.5% functions as genes that are transcribed into proteins. Other parts of the DNA that don't code for protein contain "switches" that determine which genes are activated. The function of much of the rest of the DNA molecule is unknown, and future research is certain to yield some surprises. As biologist Sean B. Carroll in Endless Forms Most Beautiful states, "The entire show involves tens of thousands of switches being thrown in sequence and in parallel." [42]

Ultimately, in each of your trillions of cells, all 20,000 genes are turned on and off in the right sequence throughout your life. Your eye never becomes a liver. In fact, throughout Nature with its millions of species, in each cell of every organism, the correct genes are activated at the correct time, in the correct sequence. Through the biochemical miracle of DNA, each cell of every organism gets it right almost all the time.

This is not merely a process that takes place in the embryo. In his Scientific American article entitled "Regulating Evolution," Carroll estimates that about 10% of our genes are active in the embryo to construct the basic body pattern. The remaining 90% are involved in the ongoing everyday processes of life. [43] When you were 5 years old, the set of genes that were active within you were appropriate for a 5-year-old. Today, a more mature set of your genes is turned on. In a biological sense, we are always a work-in-progress.

The speed and accuracy of these processes is remarkable, but not totally foolproof. During DNA replication in the unicellular bacterium E. coli, for example, enzymes line up DNA bases at the astounding rate of 1,000 bases per second, making approximately one error in every ten billion bases. [44] These occasional copying errors can result in mutations, many of which are deleterious, but not all. Such mutations might be harmful or even lethal to an individual, but over the course of immense biologic time, a rare fortuitous mutation might lead to an improvement in the fitness of an organism. [45] That is, some mutations lead to more successful organisms. It is presumed the first organisms on Earth were unicellular. The fact that life on our planet contains more than one-celled organisms or slime molds demonstrates the accumulation over time of rare favorable mutations that have given rise to increasingly complex life forms. If DNA replication were perfect every time, all organisms would still be bacteria.

Much of the early (and current) genetic research has been done on the fruit fly, Drosophila. In *Endless Forms Most Beautiful*, Sean B. Carroll describes the surprise within the scientific community when it was discovered that numerous genes found in the lowly fruit fly were found with minimal change in ourselves. A gene that triggers early development of the fruit fly's primitive heart has been found with only modest alteration to trigger development of the much more complex heart of vertebrates. A gene that initiates fruit fly leg development has been found in various structures that extend from the body of a wide range of animals: the limbs of butterflies, crustaceans, spiders and centipedes; fish fins; chicken legs. The family of genes involved in the early development of the compound insect eye of Drosophila has stayed around through the eons to begin eye formation in a wide range of species with different types of eyes, ranging from flatworms to vertebrates like us. Once nature finds a gene sequence that works, it tends to stick with it across a broad range of organisms.

63

In the words of Carroll, "… all complex animals - flies and flycatchers, dinosaurs and trilobites, butterflies and zebras and humans - share a common 'tool kit' of master genes that govern the formation and patterning of their bodies and body parts." [46] He illustrates by pointing out that 99% of human genes have a mouse counterpart, and that 96% of these genes are in the same relative order on chromosomes.

The implication is that, once such an intricate genetic mechanism develops for initiating formation of a major body part, that mechanism is preserved in species after species. Much of our human DNA therefore encodes genetic cascades shared by many species, genes from ancient epochs that remain operational and effective within us.

Yet there is clearly something new and different about our species. In her *Scientific American* article, "What Makes Us Human," biostatistician Katherine S. Pollard takes on this very question. She and Carroll note that humans and chimpanzees are identical in approximately 98.8% of DNA base pairs, differing only by 1.2% in terms of genetic endowment. [47] This certainly reflects a deep genetic kinship, though the 1.2% difference still represents about 15 million DNA base pairs. Recent studies suggest that some individuals of any species, including chimpanzees and humans, contain multiple copies of some genes rather than one copy, creating a greater individual variation in DNA both within and between species than was previously appreciated. This increases the potential difference between human and chimpanzee DNA to about 5%. The extraordinary leap humans have made as a species has occurred despite only statistically slight DNA changes.

Pollard, like Carroll, stresses the vital role of the DNA switches in determining which genes are active where. "The key story of what makes us human is probably not going to focus on changes in our protein building blocks but rather on how evolution assembled these blocks in new ways by changing when and where in the body different genes turn on and off." [48]

There are so very many problems a body must solve to be alive. It must have an effective interface between its inside and its outside; it must trap energy, sustain metabolism, maintain internal order, take in nutrients, get rid of wastes, avoid predation, reproduce. Genes provide solutions to many of these problems, honed through the ages by a process that includes the extinction of species that were not as effective or as fortunate. In each of our cells today, assembled on chains of DNA, are a collage of genes of mixed ages and remarkable histories. Some genes have existed for hundreds of millions of years, guiding the development of a wide range of species, preserved because they still effectively solve problems living organisms face. Other genes within every cell in our body are of much more recent vintage, with many influencing brain function and the flowering of intelligence that distinguishes our species. The most recent link in the genetic chain is the absolutely unique combination of genes in each one of us. There has truly never in the history of the world been another person to bring to life our personal genetic potentialities (other than an identical twin!). DNA seems magical beyond the realm of possibility, but millions upon millions of living species offer proof of its power. Watch a rose bush making roses or a bird fly. Think about the wonder of yourself.

Reproduction

Can you believe that of the millions of species on Earth, every single one can reproduce? Every living organism can not only beget the next generation, but also *pass on the code to create all future generations.*

We live in the midst of a reproductive orgy. For every currently living organism, there was a time in the past when it did not yet exist. The process of life that now animates you and me has been passed from one generation to the next over the course of eons.

Each organism is the offspring of one or more parents, and the sheer variety of reproductive methods is breathtaking. You exist because every ancestor in each generation of your direct cell line had sexual intercourse that resulted in pregnancy and childbirth. Evidently even the solemn-appearing great-grandparents in the faded photograph on your wall didn't wear those formal clothes all the time.

We are accustomed to thinking of reproduction as a sexual act, but nature uses other means as well. In fact, the majority of organisms in and on Earth are one-celled (unicellular), and most of their reproduction does not involve sex. A one-celled parent organism such as a bacterium splits into two genetically identical offspring, who in turn do the same, generation after generation. This asexual process is the commonest reproductive act on Earth, since it is the way the Earth's most numerous life forms - one-celled organisms - typically reproduce.

However, the majority of multicellular organisms (those with bodies containing more than one cell) reproduce sexually, which requires the mixing of DNA from more than one parent to produce offspring. As you might guess, most offspring of sexual reproduction contain the genetic material from two parents of different sexes. The advantage of sexual reproduction is the genetic diversity it creates. If all organisms of a species were genetically identical, any disease or toxin that killed one might kill all, because they would share the same genetic susceptibility. The commingling of DNA of parent organisms during sexual reproduction produces offspring with different combinations of genes; this increases the odds that some individuals will have the genetic programming to survive any specific challenge to the species.

If the environment becomes hotter or colder or drier or more acidic, or if infection occurs, some individuals might possess a genetic predisposition that affords higher resistance to this threat, and those would be more likely to survive and pass on to their offspring the DNA that enables them to endure. Those offspring would therefore tend to inherit and eventually pass down to their own descendants genes that increase resistance to the threat, which improves the future odds for the species. The compulsion for sexual reproduction and ultimately for species diversification is a powerful imperative with great survival value, even among species whose sex drive is purely instinctive and who do not require sexual education courses in junior high school.

Most of the organisms I see outside my window are plants whose reproductive life is complicated by being stuck immobile into the ground, forever geographically separated from their sexual mates. Courtship is certainly made more difficult by being unable to approach your sexual partner. Some plants get around this difficulty by reproducing asexually; fallen parts of a plant or cuttings or buds can sometimes grow into a normal plant genetically identical to the plant from which it came.

Plants generally do have sexual organs and most reproduce sexually; perhaps surprisingly, the majority of plants are hermaphrodites. That is, over 70 percent of plants contain both male and female sexual parts and are thus both male *and* female. The ideal sexual union for such a plant involves a complex set of relationships in which both the male and female parts of the plant find separate sexual partners. Plants produce pollen (via their stamen) as a sperm equivalent to transmit the male portion of the genome. This pollen must somehow find its way to another plant of the same species whose female organ, the ovary, produces eggs that can be fertilized by the appropriate pollen. Meanwhile, while its pollen must reach the receptive female organs of another plant, the plant's female organ, its ovary, awaits fertilization of its eggs by being on the receiving end of yet another plant's pollen. Hence with both its male and female parts forming different sexual unions, each plant can have multiple reproductive partners.

Many plants such as ragweed use the wind as their blind courier by hurling vast amounts of lightweight pollen airborne and allowing the breeze to carry it wherever it will, with the prospect that at least some of the pollen will land on a receptive ragweed and find its way to the recipient's eggs to give birth to new ragweed. The amount of pollen involved in these wind-borne transfers relies on sheer numbers to find a receptive mate, as allergy sufferers become the unwitting victims of the air-borne pollen hordes. Many species, including grasses and a variety of trees (such as conifers, oaks, walnuts, and birches), utilize this strategy of sending lightweight pollen aloft. In the picturesque language of Guy Murchie: "If the wind in the willows is a poetic phrase to you, it is assuredly even more so to the willows and many other trees, to most grasses, mushrooms and a good tenth of all flowering plants. A breeze is in truth a link in life itself for ... these graceful creatures have long found it vital to broadcast their spores wholesale to the open ocean of air around them, entrusting their descendants to the invisible rivers of wind which waft them as surely as any watery currents below - and certainly more swiftly." [49]

Plants that find more selective couriers can greatly reduce pollen production and make their sex life more efficient. An attractive flower or fragrance serves as advertising to lure a potential insect courier such as a bee. This advertising is apparently as effective as the large logo on the signs outside popular chain restaurants, drawing repeat diners over and over. The potential courier receives a reward for visiting the plant, either nutritious pollen to snack on or some sugary fluid called nectar that is produced by the plant. While dining at the plant, the courier insect brushes against the host's pollen, which sticks to it. As the courier makes its rounds among flowers of the favored species, the pollen from one plant is transmitted to another. Plants and their pollinators develop over generations a deeper relationship, in which the shapes of one adapt to the shapes of the other.

A pollinator doesn't receive a full meal at any stop, which would reduce its interest in visiting other plants. Rather it receives a small feeding at each, forcing it to visit and pollinate many plants over the course of the day. Some pollinators are generalists - they are willing to dine at a variety of plants. Such generalists are not ideal from the plant's point of view, because they may deliver the pollen of one species to the wrong address, to plants of a different species. On the other hand, some species of orchid or rose develop specific relationships with a very discriminating species of pollinators, whose shapes adapt precisely to their particular consorts.

Many species of birds are also pollinators, intermediaries in the sex lives of plants. Hummingbirds and a variety of tropical nectar-feeding birds serve this function. Cacti, so forbidding during the day, often open their flowers overnight to offer their nectar to pollinating bats.

Plants generally minimize the amount of self-fertilization between the male and female organs of the same plant. Perhaps the organs are separated in space or mature at different times. The survival benefit is greatly enhanced if genes are shared between different organisms rather than merely utilized in a self-fertilization. Yet some pioneer species of plant that find themselves without nearby mates do have the ability to self-fertilize and keep the species alive until other plants arrive for cross-fertilization.

Plants package seeds in tasty fruits to be eaten and excreted, or enclosed in nuts to be buried, scattering seeds of a new generation. When we carry pesky burrs on our socks after hiking in the woods, we are taking our part in the reproductive life of plants by carrying their seeds. It seems amazing that such a system works. Not only does the plant require sunlight, water, and key nutrients from the earth, but also an ecosystem that sustains appropriate pollinators. Every living thing requires a sustaining system of relationships with the environment around it.

Animal reproduction tends to follow patterns more familiar to us. There is a price animals pay when they store the male's sperm and the female's eggs in relatively safe locations within the body. In many species, such as mammals, for male and female sexual cells (gametes) to meet requires essentially a body to body (or body into body) close encounter, with all its inherent risks. Courtships can become elaborate, mate choice critical. One party must overcome caution to try to lure the other sex into physical closeness, hoping that any sexual displays will impress the intended target without drawing the unwanted attention of outsiders such as predators. In quest of mates with which to merge genes, Ursula Goodenough, professor of biology at Washington University in St. Louis, says, "Fireflies pulse, houseflies beat their wings, moths send out musk, fish dance, frogs croon, birds display feathers and song, mammals strut and preen." [50] These displays are going on all around us.

Ornithologist and ecologist Robert Ricklefs points out that, "It is a basic asymmetry of nature that a female's evolutionary fitness depends on her ability to make eggs and otherwise provide for her offspring, whereas a male's fitness usually depends on the number of matings he can procure." After providing the sperm to initiate pregnancy, the male contribution to the offspring's future ranges from deep commitment to total neglect. He may move on to impregnate multiple females with a "love them and leave them" approach or, in some species, may be strictly monogamous. Ricklefs summarizes, "Among animal taxa as a whole, promiscuous mating is by far the commonest system, and it is universal among outcrossing plants." [51]

Romance is unlikely to be a key factor in the mating of black widow spiders and praying mantises, two species in which the female often devours the male during the mating process. Many fish species also avoid the romance part through the process of external fertilization, in which females eject clouds of eggs and males eject clouds of sperm that commingle and fertilize each other in the ocean. This external fertilization is maximized if members of the species cluster together to create a mass coordinated mutual release of sperm and eggs. It is often uncertain what environmental or internal cues trigger mass mating conventions in which widespread members of a species congregate, disseminate the sperm and eggs that hold their genetic future, and then scatter back through the oceans. Schools of fish tend to be of mixed sexes, a natural bunching that lends itself readily to cross-fertilization through which members of the school share in orgies of egg and sperm release into the ocean. As Guy Murchie says, "In fact one might say the whole school is 'going steady' with itself all the time." [52]

Among fish there are other reproductive strategies. In many species, such as the bluegill sunfish, males defend spawning territories to which they attempt to attract females. The males then guard and defend the eggs against predators, while also attempting to ward off opportunistic males trying to sneak copulations with females within that territory. Such behavior is presumably instinctive, part of the lifelong battle to pass on genes to future generations in an environment laden with predators and competitors.

Romance is a very late arrival in what had been an ancient and loveless process of reproduction. For much of Earth's reproductive history, an effective strategy was to generate massive numbers of offspring, enough to survive high mortality rates, including the certainty that many immature life forms make easy snacks for predators. Having millions of offspring does not lend itself to emotional relationships between parent and child.

One large group of insects is named Hymenoptera, containing wasps, bees, and ants (over 130,000 species have been identified). If this group were to institute sex education classes, the information would seem particularly puzzling to us. Females make eggs, which if left unfertilized develop into males. If those same eggs are fertilized by combining them with sperm, the resultant individuals become females. Improbably, the addition of sperm to an unfertilized egg turns that individual, which would otherwise have become a male, into a female. Ricklefs states, "Reproductive females control the sex ratio of the offspring simply by using sperm stored when they mate to fertilize eggs, thereby producing females, or not, thereby producing males." [53] Fertile females must somehow evaluate the needs of the collective group and then determine whether the group's needs are better served by additional males or additional females. The sex of the next ant or bee that you see was determined by whether a fertile female of the prior generation chose to add or withhold sperm to the egg that housed this particular insect.

In many sexual organisms, such as humans, the commonest male:female ratio is about 1:1. Each offspring in such species has one mother and one father. Should the next generation contain significantly more of one sex than the other, sexual competition in the next generation should even the ratio. That is, individuals of the rarer sex will be more likely to mate because they will face less competition from the relatively few other members of their sex. On the other hand, individuals of the sex with excess members will face more mating competition and be less likely to find sexual partners and reproduce. In fact, the human sex ratio at birth is approximately 105 male births per 100 female births. Cultural policies, such as warfare, can temporarily skew the ratio, and women tend to dominate at higher age demographics due to their longer life expectancy.

There also exist species that change sexes over the course of their lives. The slipper shell, Crepidula, is a sperm-producing male when young and small, then develops into an egg-producing female when older and larger. Wrasses, reef-inhabiting fish, tend to mate as females when young. As they grow larger and can more effectively compete for potential mates, they become males.

Among many species, survival of the young is improved if they are given parental protection. In an environment in which every organism is a potential meal for a predator, eggs and nearly defenseless newborns are a common food source. In our own species, a mutual monogamous bond commonly develops between parents, who have relatively few offspring compared to many of nature's species, but typically stay together to nurture those offspring for years. Infant survival is optimized by having two parental guardians in frequent attendance, a system also employed by many species of birds. Since either bird parent can sit on eggs to warm and guard them, and since either parent can retrieve tasty worms for feeding infants, such tasks can be shared.

While mating pairs of humans and numerous bird species tend to develop monogamous bonds that can last till death, such relationships are not widespread throughout the animal kingdom, or even throughout the realm of mammals. Female mammals carry the unborn infants within their bodies and feed them breast milk after birth, leading to a greater female role in child-rearing, while the male after contributing sperm has no further biological mandate toward an infant he has spawned. In many species, males are promiscuous, sending their DNA into the future via many copulations, but not reducing their reproductive opportunities by settling down with any given female. Viewed over the entire range of animals, this promiscuous male reproductive strategy is the commonest.

Another common strategy is polygamy, in which a male forms long-term relationships with numerous members of the other sex. Within his territory, the male claims sexual access to the females in return for protecting the females and their offspring against predators.

Humans, though primarily monogamous, have had historical eras of polygamy, and still have polygamous ethnic groups today. For that matter, many human matings are promiscuous, in which the father after impregnating the female withdraws from further involvement. Polygamy was common in Biblical times but does induce certain instabilities into a culture. For example, it is alleged that Biblical King Solomon, reputed to be the world's wisest man, had 700 wives and 300 concubines. In a monogamous society, those 1,000 women would provide mates for 1,000 men. In King Solomon's era, 999 men would be deprived of mates because King Solomon claimed them all.

Since the human male:female ratio approximates 1:1, any polygamous male deprives another male of a mate. This creates a group of outcast males who are unable to find mates within the culture, creating among them a sense of disenfranchisement, which can become a source of civil unrest. Monogamy is the system that maximizes the number of men with mates by preventing the rich and powerful from claiming more than one. Perhaps there are many women who would rather be the 50th wife of a billionaire than the only wife of an impoverished farmer, but most billionaires are claimed in matrimony early and not currently available. Monogamy in a sense reduces the number of offspring that billionaires can have by limiting the number of legal mates to one.

In nature, there are parallels to these sorts of relationships. For example, redwing blackbird males tend to settle around lakes, with earlier-arriving and stronger birds claiming the best habitats and defending them, leaving poorer habitats for late-comers. As females return, they preferentially settle and mate in the best available habitats with the stronger males until all the strong males and best habitats are taken. At this point, any females who arrive later must choose between becoming one of multiple mates for a strong male in a good habitat, or the sole mate for a weaker male in a poorer habitat. Each female must then weigh which type of setting will maximize her chances of successful mating. Humans by law in most societies no longer have this choice, seeking out an acceptable mate only among those who are currently unmated.

The qualities that make potential mates attractive vary among species, though the commonest pattern in nature is for males to flaunt their sex appeal, while females then choose which male they find most desirable for mating. Males of numerous species historically had to battle each other for turf and for access to females, so superior size and strength often trumped other factors in mate choice and led to males becoming larger than females in many species. In such battles, size definitely matters. Commonly, though, males have the showiest plumage, the most dramatic vocalizations, the snazziest dances, the gaudiest beaks and tails, in hopes that these displays will lure females to choose them. Flashing fireflies, chirping insects, and croaking frogs are all at least partly advertising their sexuality.

As you look around at the life forms in nature, recognize that each has a pedigree in a sense as remarkable as your own. Every direct ancestor of each living organism survived long enough to successfully procreate. Each unwanted and unloved weed demonstrates that for thousands and thousands of years, gusts of wind or the irregular flight of pollinators successfully transferred pollen from one of its ancestors to another. The commingled DNA was then inserted into more pollen to entrust to new generations of insects or fresh breezes, on and on to the present day. Each lizard, sparrow, and squirrel packaged its DNA into a transmissible form and then instinctively acted to deliver that DNA into other organisms to direct the synthesis of future bodies through the centuries.

If reproduction were rare, its miraculous nature would be obvious. If only one organism were capable of reproducing, we would observe it in awe. Current estimates of the total species count on Earth range from a few million to perhaps 100 or more million, and every species has found a method to reproduce and generate continually new organisms of its kind. The variety of reproductive strategies is staggering. Some organisms split in half, some change sex over the course of their life, some devour their mates. Some organisms smash heads in combat for the right to reproduce. With or without sexuality, with or without pollen and wind, with or without ongoing relationships between mates, with or without fragrances, with or without gaudy feathers, in dry deserts and dark oceans, each type of organism acts in a way to pass its genes into the future. Animals under the influence of compulsive instinctive drives they likely don't understand are driven to mate and beget the future of their species in every era. As you look at any living being, consider its long list of ancestors who each found a way to procreate.

The mating behavior of our human species is no longer so completely based on instinct as the squirrel or lizard, but we have not totally moved beyond instinct either. Our courtships may last months or years instead of seconds or minutes, as we seek soul mates rather than merely reproductive partners. Further, while many organisms in nature time their mating and gestation to give birth during favorable warm seasons when abundant plant life supports a richer ecosystem, humans mate year-round unfettered by seasonal change. We do certainly use hair and clothing styles and makeup to advertise our suitability, and our behavior can tip off potential mates regarding our availability. Contraceptive technology has now allowed a disconnect between sexual intercourse and reproduction. Instinctive physical sexual drives, emotional attachment for sexual partners, and reproduction itself have all been potentially separated.

When one-celled organisms divided in half, or schools of fish spilled out clouds of sperms and eggs, the process of reproduction presumably had nothing to do with emotional attachment. Somewhere along the way, there arose coupling relationships that lasted beyond the process of intercourse, beyond even the relatively short-term stage of protecting vulnerable infants from carnivores. The possibility developed that mating individuals could develop love for each other, love for their offspring, love for the parents who gave birth to them and the siblings who were raised with them. Of all the reproductive processes on our planet, the development of a protective emotional attachment of mates for each other and their offspring is a new and startling development. Out of eons of reproductive history in which the miracle lay in the biochemical processes and instinctive drives that led each species to generate new organisms of its kind, there arose this miracle among miracles, the binding emotion of love.

Take away love, and the conflict so inherent in the world of nature becomes the dominant theme of life. Love toward a mate, toward family, has the chance to spread outward into the world, to friends, to new people we meet, perhaps to those whom we haven't met. Love provides a positive connection between beings instead of a competitive one and raises the possibility of a different story line for human life. We bind ourselves to what we love, and the richness of our life is largely in the richness of those loves. Even impersonal loves such as passion for a place or an activity enrich us. Should we minimize our loves, we hurl ourselves into the competitive battles for survival and advancement, to loveless biochemistry and instinct, and the quest for material possessions that never love us back.

We cohabit the world with organisms as ancient and as new as ourselves. Unlike most of these organisms, we live with the possibility of love, of imbuing our relationships with richness. We add to the meaning and fullness of our lives by what we choose to touch with love. Let us use this magic wand to give meaning to our relationships with each other, and with this wondrous planet and its ability to draw from the ancient the eternally new. Take the further step of looking into the eyes of someone you love.

Recycling, Cosmic Style

The sunlight that pours down on Earth is continually new, forged by the fusion of hydrogen to helium. As the sunlight warms your skin, you can be aware that it left that most precious of stars 93 million miles and eight minutes ago. Our ecosystems need that daily infusion of energy. For example, if a lawn is deprived of sunlight for a couple of weeks during the growing season, the grass dies. The energy from sunlight fuels almost the entire food chain.

On the other hand, there is no similar infusion of freshly minted atoms on our planet to make new living bodies. Earth is finite, so bodies can only be created from recycled materials that have been part of our planet or its atmosphere for its entire 4.6 billion-year history. The same elements move around and change attachments over the course of seconds, hours, and eons to generate every form you currently see.

In the words of Lawrence University geology professor Marcia Bjornerud, "Carbon, water, sulfur, phosphorus, and nitrogen are in constant motion at and near the Earth's surface, reincarnated again and again as minerals in rocks, gases in the atmosphere, ions in the ocean, schools of fish, leaves on trees" [54] – and, of course, as our own bodies. Sunlight eight minutes old stirs the ancient chemicals of Earth into an endless variety of new and transient forms. Bjornerud continues, "Nothing is unusable waste, and nothing will last forever, at least not in any particular form. Matter resides temporarily in various lodging places, then moves on in new guises." [55]

The carbon and oxygen atoms that are in your lungs for perhaps a few seconds now may have spent millions of years in the rock of the Earth and the air of its atmosphere before becoming a temporary part of you. The carbon dioxide you are now breathing out will likely not stay in the atmosphere very long before entering the leaves of a plant, perhaps to be passed on as a future meal for a herbivore, and then through countless unknown future transformations. No forms are permanent; all are transient combinations of ancient atoms that each have long separate histories before being drawn together into their current set of attachments we call a flower or dog - or our "self."

Dr. Michael Wysession puts it like this, "There are atoms right now in your body that were in dinosaurs, that were in volcanoes, that were once in the body of Julius Caesar, that have flowed out of the mouth of the Nile River many, many times." [56] On the one hand, one can recognize the role of DNA as the choreographer that arranges these atoms into alignment within bodies that translate chemistry into life. Yet, as previously mentioned, the atoms of DNA are constantly in flux, like all earthly forms, so even molecules of DNA are composed of different atoms today than yesterday.

Look at every form you see around you. Imagine the complex history of every atom. With each meal, you incorporate new atoms into yourself in exchange for outgoing atoms that had previously been a part of you. Your form remains pretty much the same and so does your identity, but the atoms themselves are in flux, traded back and forth between you and the planet. You are a work continually in progress, newly in the process of being assembled at every moment, and so is the world around you. The "you" that is reading this sentence has never existed before. Celebrate the uniqueness of yourself and this moment.

Nature recycles too, though the time between disappearance and reappearance can vary from milliseconds to eons, and the atoms making up the original thing may come back as parts of many different things, continually remixed and recycled again and again. In fact, every meal represents a recycling of chemicals and stored energy from one life form to another.

All organisms must perform transformations to survive. The main energy input into the Earth's ecosystem is sunlight, trapped by plants through photosynthesis. It is estimated that only 1-2% of the sunlight that strikes our planet is captured as energy via the photosynthetic process. [57] Much of the sunlight strikes parts of the planetary surface covered with pavement or dirt, or parts of a plant such as branches or stems where photosynthesis is not performed. There are inefficiencies within the photosynthetic process itself, and energy is lost at each chemical transformation associated with an organism's metabolism. Further, it is approximated that about 90% of energy is lost with each transformation between trophic levels, from plant to herbivore to carnivore. Yet that daily allotment of sunlight is our planet's main paycheck, which wouldn't support a large ecosystem were it not continually reinvested.

The sunlight we receive today is not, however, our only energy source. While plants can draw their energy directly from today's sunlight, the energy from sunlight must be recycled to support animals that eat the plants and animals that eat the animals that eat the plants. The same energy from prior sunlight is passed from organism to organism, recycled, and added to today's sunlight to fuel our ecosystem. Further, fossil fuels contain the energy of ancient sunlight that plants eons ago trapped via photosynthesis before being buried and removed from the food chain, as their bodies, compressed over deep time, turned to the coal and oil that heat our homes and fuel our vehicles.

For all non-photosynthesizers such as ourselves, we must find a steady supply of organisms that have managed to trap or recycle that solar energy, and we must eat them to turn their energy into our energy and their atoms into our atoms. Plants are eaten by herbivores, which are eaten by carnivores, with plant atoms and energy becoming herbivore atoms and energy before being recycled into carnivore atoms and energy. Ultimately, eating by each animal is the act of incorporating the atoms and stored energy of another organism into itself. David Suzuki adds an ironic twist: "In nature, the difference between the diners and the dined upon may be just a matter of time." [58]

In all animals, many of the atoms from prior meals are now a part of their bodies. At the time of death, each organism puts its chemicals and residual energy back into the biological bank of the Earth, to be withdrawn and transformed again.

Because terrestrial plants have evolved defenses such as woody branches and thorns, these plants are surprisingly effective at repulsing full-scale consumption by herbivores. The branched structure of plants also affords protection so that part of the plant, like a leaf or branch, can be eaten, yet the plant survives. Hence trees live decades or centuries, and your neighbor's rosebush with its defensive thorns is still going strong. When a tree or plant eventually dies, it is the so-called decomposers or detritus feeders that play the largest role in recycling their stored energy.

Eventually all living things on this finite planet die, and their energy, nutrients, and minerals would be lost like a bad investment in a bankrupt company were it not for organisms whose very names chill our spine. Dead trees are eaten and their energy and molecules recycled by organisms such as termites, millipedes, and fungi. Bacteria feast within the soil on each other and on the bodies of dead organisms of all types, and are in turn feasted upon.

To again quote Ricklefs, "Ninety percent or more of the plant biomass produced in forested habitats passes through the detritus reservoir. The nutrients locked up in detritus are regenerated into forms that can be used by the activities of the countless worms, snails, insects, mites, bacteria, and fungi that consume detritus - their primary source of carbon and energy - as food." [59] Then perhaps the same nutrients might take flight within a bird that dines on the worms and insects that consume the detritus.

The magician, the planet Earth - call it any name you wish - takes the residua of everything that ever existed, stirs it with fresh energy from the sun, and constantly creates the new world of this moment with its myriad forms. You are a hybrid in which atoms that have been in living organisms many times before and which come from countless different sources have been recycled and merged into your living, thinking, amazing self. Each animal is likewise a composite of atoms from many sources, atoms that have been part of multiple prior living things, atoms that now compose perhaps a dog or a chipmunk. No organism is a bounded, discrete entity enclosed by skin. Each is an open process, continuously transforming the ecological web of Earth and transformed by it.

Molecules that were in the supermarket yesterday that you ingest with tonight's dinner will be part of your body tomorrow. Eat mindfully, with reverence.

Death

Death waits for all of us, and we know it. It picks off, one by one, people who are precious to us as we wait our turn. It is the ultimate personal tragedy, an inescapable part of being human.

Greek mythology envisioned the outcome if it were possible to circumvent human death. The goddess Eos (Roman: Aurora), who possessed eternal life, asked Zeus to grant immortality to her mortal lover Tithonus. Zeus complied, but Eos neglected to include eternal youth as part of her request. Tithonus lived on, becoming progressively older and enfeebled in mind and body. According to Homer, Eos put Tithonus in a room to continue his downhill course forever, and there she left him.   Eternal life without eternal youth proved to be a catastrophe rather than a blessing.

Yet for the great majority of living organisms on our planet, death is not inevitable. The combination of eternal life and eternal youth turns out to be the commonest reproductive pattern on Earth. The catch is that the apparently fortunate organisms that are able to cheat death are single-celled. These unicellular organisms not only vastly outnumber but also far outweigh all multicellular organisms combined. [60] That is, the life forms we visually behold, like trees and whales and ants and people, make up a small part of the biosphere compared to single-celled organisms. To see these potentially immortal one-celled beings (such as bacteria), look at a sample from almost anywhere through a microscope.

While unicellular organisms certainly can die, their usual fate is to divide into two daughter cells that are identical to the parent cell, and those daughter cells likewise divide into two offspring, and so on.   Natural environments in reality lack the resources to support eternal growth, but it is not part of the intrinsic nature of such unicellular organisms to grow old and expire. Any of these single-celled organisms can die of heat or cold, of drought or exposure to toxic chemicals, of exhausting its resources or losing the battle for an ecological niche in nature. However, if circumstances that support their life persist, unicellular organisms keep reproducing and don't die. From the perspective of DNA, by clothing itself within one-celled organisms theoretically capable of reproducing indefinitely and making copies of the parent cell's DNA with each replication, the DNA is carried into the future inside the bodies of continually replicating, potentially eternal host organisms.

Further, the first organisms on Earth were unicellular, and for a large part of the planet's history, the only life forms were unicellular. The Earth is about four and a half billion years old, and one-celled organisms are thought to have first developed three to four billion years ago. It is speculated that they were the only life on Earth for a billion or more years. At some point, it is presumed a one-celled organism divided into two, but the two daughter cells didn't separate, and the dawn of multicellular organisms had arrived. As more cells divided but stuck together, larger and more complex life forms developed over the eons. The dates are murky because one-celled organisms don't form fossils (nor in general do other soft tiny beings). Clearly documented fossils of multicellular organisms from 550 to 670 million years ago have been found, but fossils as old as 2 billion years are also felt by some researchers to be multicellular.

The point is that over the billion or more years in which all earthly life forms were unicellular, death of an individual organism was possible but not inevitable. Through repetitive division into daughter cells, immortality of a sort was the norm for life on Earth. In fact, for the one-celled organisms that still are the numerically dominant life forms today, that possibility of immortality still exists.

But not for us. Multicellular organisms brought a new degree of complexity into the world and also brought genetically programmed inevitable death. Evolution is not soft and sentimental - organisms only survive if they out-compete other living beings for a particular ecological niche. Those traits that aid survival of the species will be preserved. If the development of complexity brought with it the inevitability of death in those complex organisms, the question is raised whether the inevitable death of individuals serves a benefit for the species. Guy Murchie affirms this idea and calls it the "...realization that mortality has survival value that progressively evolved out of immortality...." [61]

There is a reason professional football teams do not hire 90-year-old players. They are slow and fragile compared to 25-year-olds. A team with multiple 90-year-olds would be first only in career-ending injuries or worse. To remain successful, teams continually replace past-peak players with younger ones, especially if losing teams are eliminated and only winners advance.

Organisms not only compete with other species but also compete with other members of their own species. Presuming that an ecological niche has limited resources, old and feeble organisms that consume them would reduce access to those resources by younger and fitter individuals of their species, dragging down the whole species.

Further, complex organisms can't achieve immortality through simple repetitive cell division. A one-celled amoeba just divides and then divides again. A mammal cannot simply churn out more and more of every type of cell to stay forever fresh and competitive. In higher organisms, only malignant cells keep dividing relentlessly.

In this context, multicellular organisms can be thought of as containing two categories of cell, a mortal part and a small but potentially immortal part. This division applies whether we consider plants or animals, so it would apply to essentially any organism you see out your window. One category consists of specialized reproductive or "germ cells," which are involved in sexual reproduction and contain genetic information that is potentially immortal. (The phrase "germ cells" when describing reproduction has the same root as "germinal" or "germinate" and nothing to do with germs that cause infections.) The other category, somatic cells, makes up all the rest of an animal or plant's body. Your somatic cells include your heart, lungs, muscles, bones, arms, legs, liver, kidneys, digestive tract, and brain – the mortal part of you. In humans, the germ cells are within the ovaries and testes, and the somatic cells are the rest of your body. The precious genes that are passed down through the generations are transmitted by the DNA in germ cells, and many of these genes are only minimally changed through the course of millions of years. That is, the genetic information encoded in the DNA of germ cells can be transmitted through the eons if that DNA generates organisms that are reproductively successful.

As Ursula Goodenough, puts it, "But once you have a life cycle with a germ line and a soma, then immortality is handed over to the germ line." [62] The soma (or body) is then freed to maximally adapt to ecological niches, and in doing so "... generated every complex morphological structure imaginable: wings, gills, eyes, leaves, glands, claws, bark, nostrils, tentacles." [63] If these adaptations are successful, the soma will offer the means by which the DNA patterns in germ cells can be passed on to the next generation.

In a sense, this can be viewed as the story of DNA. It can also be told as the story of evolution through the generation of an endless variety of body structures, which if successful, allow survival of the organism and transmission of its DNA. There are millions upon millions of species on Earth, each representing the means by which particular arrangements of DNA make their way through the present into the future.

A huge component of this story of multicellular organisms becomes the saga of sex, for it is the sex cells like those in human ovaries and testes that are carriers of the potentially eternal DNA patterns that encode the next generation of bodies, and through that next generation, the possibility of all future generations. Through the mixing of DNA from separate individuals via sexual reproduction, a more diverse population is created, increasing the odds that some of those individuals will be well enough suited to a changing environment to survive and pass on their DNA.

That DNA travels generation by generation via a relay composed of mortal bodies that are each equipped to play their role in transmitting potentially eternal information encoded within DNA before meeting their own individual demise. It should come as no surprise that the sex drive is so powerful, when sexual interaction between organisms is the means by which potentially eternal DNA patterns pass to the next generation. Body chemistry, hormones, and brain connections act in concert up and down the animal kingdom to an overpowering level, as if the future of the species depends upon sex, which it does.

But what about our bodies? If we can't be immortal, why can't we live 1,000 years or so, like Methuselah? The answer to the question, and the explanation for the doom that awaits our bodies, comes from the problem of trying to adapt to a changing set of conditions in the world. If there were no programmed death in a particular species, if the body were potentially eternal, that body would not be able to adapt to changing environmental conditions because it would be locked into its original form. Such a species, unable to quickly adjust to changes in environmental niches, would be out-competed by species with limited individual life spans that kept handing off the DNA to new and better-adapted individuals. Nature takes care of this by programming death into each multicellular organism after it has lived long enough to transmit DNA, so that a fresh, young next generation provides a new if temporary home for its potentially eternal DNA patterns. The faster the environment is changing, the greater the stress on old forms that no longer fit, and the greater the reward for species of limited life spans that allow quicker adaptation.

In nature, a species whose individuals might live a million years would be driven to extinction by species with genetically programmed mortality that continually produce new generations armed with nature's latest innovations, such as faster legs, sharper teeth, or smarter brains. It would be like pitting an automobile from 1897 against one made within the last year in a winner-take-all race (even if we take decrepitude out of the equation by presuming that the 1897 car has been perfectly maintained and runs as well as it did in 1897, at 28 miles per hour).

Unfortunately for us as perceptive humans, the death of individuals is part of the mechanism by which species continually re-optimize. Even species themselves are not eternal and are subject to extinction because entire species can be locked into forms that lose the competition within nature's ecological niches. It is estimated that well over 99% of species that ever existed are now extinct, as the lineup card of life keeps changing.

The world without genetically programmed death is the world of one-celled microorganisms, which mindlessly conduct their internal biochemistry and ultimately divide in two, serving basically as DNA copying machines. One bacterium containing DNA divides into two bacteria, each containing a copy of DNA identical to the parent cell. Wouldn't you hope the Earth offered more to life than that? Our entire beautiful world of complex organisms has been wrought by the continual birth of new life in trade for old life whose time has come and passed.

To again quote Ursula Goodenough: "Death is the price to be paid to have trees and clams and birds and grasshoppers, and death is the price paid to have human consciousness, to be aware of all that shimmering awareness and all that love. My somatic life is the wondrous gift wrought by my forthcoming death." [64]

In Don DeLillo's novel, *White Noise*, one of the characters is haunted by a fear of death. This prompts another character to say, "... I think it's a mistake to lose one's sense of death, even one's fear of death. Isn't death the boundary we need? Doesn't it give a precious texture to life, a sense of definition? You have to ask yourself whether anything you do in this life would have beauty and meaning without the knowledge you carry of a final line, a border or limit." [65]

Despite its terrible toll on each of us personally, death is partly the architect of the beautiful and complex world we share. It is the eraser that removed dinosaurs and trilobites and millions of other species to open the world for Homo sapiens and its remarkable brain. With its dance partner Birth, Death continually sweeps away the old to allow the creativity of Earth to express itself in new and wondrous life forms. The amazing complexity of human beings with all their passions, the entire evolutionary climb from potentially eternal but ultimately mindless one-celled life, is our debt to Birth and Sex and Death dancing to the rhythms of the Earth. All multicellular organisms are dancers.

It is thought that our universe came into being in a single creation event. Everything that currently exists - including ourselves - represents transformations of that original "stuff." That is, the physical ingredients of which we are made are as old as the universe, currently estimated at 13.7 billion years. Viewed in that way, we and everything around us are composed of material from the dawn of the universe, transformed over and over. Somewhere along the way, DNA began directing the transformations of earthly chemicals into living organisms. Here we are, celebrating our 13.7 billionth birthday, passionately alive. Cosmologist Joel R. Primack and scientist/lawyer/philosopher Nancy Ellen Abrams put it like this, "Every particle in our bodies has a multibillion-year past, every cell and every bodily organ has a multimillion-year past, and many of our ways of thinking have multithousand-year pasts. Each of us is a nerve center where these various cosmic histories intersect." [66]

If we are a magic trick by which DNA furthers its own ends, we are still magic. It is partly the awareness of our eventual death that shines a spotlight on our life. Because there is a limit to our number of days, each day becomes a special and glorious opportunity to be alive. We must be aware that the consciousness that is our special gift is at least partly due to the creativity death imposes on a fertile sun-drenched planet.

Life as "Disequilibrium"

There is a word to describe the state of bodies in perfect chemical equilibrium with the outside world. That state is called "Death." For all organisms, being alive requires the ability to maintain within the body an internal environment that differs from the external one, a disequilibrium. This in turn requires energy, which must be harvested from the outside to maintain an organism's unique order on the inside.

For example, nitrogen makes up about 78% of our atmosphere but only 3% of our body. Although water, consisting of two hydrogen atoms and one oxygen atom, composes half to two-thirds of our body, hydrogen is "less than a quarter of one percent of solid Earth...." [67] All known living organisms of Earth are referred to as "carbon-based life forms" - this element, so essential to the biochemistry of life, makes up less than one-fifth of one percent of our planet, but 18% of our body. [68] Trace quantities of iron within our hemoglobin have the critical role of carrying oxygen to all our cells, but our bodies make essentially no use of the silicon that constitutes about 28% of Earth's crust.

While all living things are formed from the elements of our planet and its atmosphere, clearly fish are not just a bag of seawater, and we are not merely a bag of dirt. Living organisms extract and maintain concentrations of elements within their bodies that are very different from their relative ratios in the

87

outside world, an ongoing chemical disequilibrium. Further, on the coldest winter day, we burn internally at an average temperature of 98.6°, far warmer than the outside air.

Our bodies are internally subdivided by membranes that act as fences, demarcating us into organs that sustain a chemical uniqueness on one side of the fence compared to the other. Within cells, pumps eject chemicals whose concentration within the cell must be kept low. Atoms on the outside of the cell probe for "gates" in cell membranes that act like discreet doormen at a private club, allowing entry to the right elements while denying entry to others. Pumps turn on and off; gates open and close.

The function of our nerve cells (neurons), for example, requires preparation by generating high concentrations of sodium outside the cell and high potassium inside, so that the nerve is primed like a drawn bow to spring into action. Cellular pumps accomplish this setup, this imbalance. When a nerve is activated, the properties of the nerve change, and selective gates in the cell membrane open, sending the massed sodium and potassium ions rushing across the membrane to transmit the impulse from one end of the neuron to the other.

Kidneys play a vital role in maintaining the correct composition of the body. Membranes within the kidneys continually change their properties to determine which chemicals that previously were part of our self should now be evicted and which ones should be embraced to continue as part of "me." Based on differences in our dietary intake and metabolism, the composition of fluid entering the kidneys varies. The kidneys must then triage the various chemicals flowing through them, excreting almost all of some, while retaining many others, and opening the floodgates to release the right amount of water to keep the level in the body stable. The concentration of particular elements within the body and within specific organs and cells differs greatly from the chemistry of the outside world, and the kidneys, by guarding the exit, almost always keep our internal levels within a narrow normal range.

Kidneys don't function alone; like other parts of the body, they are interwoven into a larger whole. Different sensors within the body monitor fluid and chemical levels, and convey feedback to the kidneys. In particular, the pituitary gland by its secretion into the bloodstream of anti-diuretic hormone (ADH) sends instructions to the kidney membranes regarding how much water to excrete, definitely more after the third glass of tea or beer. Check the last lab work your doctor ordered for you; you should be impressed by how many of your chemistries are in the normal range, regardless of the variations in your diet and activities. Your kidneys likely did an excellent job.

The stomach is an important entryway into the body and must dutifully screen candidates for admittance. Healthy food must be allowed in, germs kept out. Primitive man lacked a working refrigerator and often ate food heavily laden with bacteria that could cause disease. This remains a problem in parts of the world that lack refrigeration or fresh food even today. The body literally provides an "acid test" of worthiness on all applicants for oral entry by maintaining within the stomach high acid levels to kill many of the incoming bacteria. This potentially toxic acid, quite capable of burning tissues, acts like a customs checkpoint on an international border.

Ulcer victims are not so happy about this acidity when it burns the lining of their digestive tract, and they may choose to take medication to prevent the acidity or block its effects on tissue. Since refrigerated fresh food is unlikely to be heavily laden with germs, lowering the stomach acidity with medication in our current cultural environment does not usually lead to recurrent digestive infections, but the natural process of creating high stomach acidity served a valuable role in our forebears. It still serves that role in parts of the world that do not have access to a sanitized food supply, and in many animals.

Since the main chemical reactions of all bodies, whether plant or animal or even one-celled, require that the chemicals be dissolved in water before they can enter life-sustaining processes, maintaining an appropriate internal concentration of water is a universal need of living organisms (even in a desert!). Plants wilt when they become low in water, and humans develop thirst. Neither cattle drinking from a pond nor humans drinking from a water fountain have performed conscious calculations regarding the concentration of their internal chemicals that drives them to ingest more water. We have a drink, our blood concentration of chemicals normalizes, and our sense of thirst resolves.

Hunger serves as notice for the need to add nutrients, as well as calories, for fueling our metabolic processes. Maintaining a body with a temperature of 98.6° and sustaining a chemical disequilibrium with the outside world requires energy. We obtain that energy from the food we eat, and hunger reminds us of this need. Our forebears were undoubtedly lured to high calorie foods to ward off starvation. We have inherited the genetic predisposition to favor high calorie foods, though we sometimes don't wait for a hunger trigger. Sometimes mere habit or even boredom will suffice.

We do require that our diet incorporate all the elements needed to assemble our body. Just think of the complexity required for probing the products of the Earth (and air) for all the chemicals necessary to make a body, determining the proper ratio of those chemicals, obtaining the chemicals through diet (and breathing), adding the right amount of water to keep the concentrations correct, dissolving the right amount of those chemicals to allow the appropriate metabolic reactions within the body, excreting any excesses, and then modulating the reactions so that life continues. Amazingly, with its system of sensors and its specialized organs, our body performs all of this. Equally amazing, every fish and kangaroo performs these same functions. Each plant extracts from the Earth the nutrients needed for life, ignoring many commoner elements while selecting the essential ones. Plants obtain the energy to maintain this chemical disequilibrium with their environment by utilizing solar energy instead of dietary energy sources.

Eventually bodies lose the ability to sustain their disequilibrium with the environment, and that marks the end of their earthly life with all its satisfactions and tribulations. Only after death does chemical equilibrium come to an organism. Till then, each of us is subject to hungers, thirsts, sex drives, fears, and a host of complex emotions. The emotions of disequilibrium are a part of every life and do not make us flawed. Despite the brilliance of our body in assembling chemicals and giving them life, we are manifestations of disequilibrium and have drives and emotions that reflect this basic reality. Our desire for psychological tranquility exists against the backdrop of metabolic and physiological need. We are not at chemical peace with the outside world or contentedly self-contained. Instead we have the imperfect miracle we call life.

Emergence

Emergence is a word used to denote that a collection of parts can have a dramatically higher level of organization than would be evident in thinking merely about the individual parts. To pick a simple example, consider that a culture is composed of individuals. Without people, the culture would not exist. However, meeting a lot of individual people might not be adequate to predict the nature of the culture. Psychologists could explore individual behavior, and sociologists could study group behavior, and both realms of study would be valid - but incomplete. Neither could accurately predict from one scale of behavior (individual versus group) the complete truth of the other scale.

Emergence leaps the chasm between pre-existing smaller parts and a new whole made up of those parts. It is the bridge across some of the greatest mysteries in the universe. The earliest mystery, the origin of the universe, may or may not have been an example of emergence in this sense. On our side of the bridge is the universe of which we are a part. What, if anything, was on the other side of the bridge? Was there a Creator? Is there something about the potentiality of seemingly empty space that can bubble up into a universe? Was there a pre-existing Something, part of which became our universe? Emergence in the sense of greater complexity arising from less complex parts may or may not have played a role in this original mystery.

Then there was a universe, made of lifeless matter. Chemicals reacted with each other to form new chemicals, over and over again. Then somewhere, sometime, from collections of chemicals, there emerged living organisms. The lifeless chemicals were necessary to form living bodies, but the development of life was in no way an obviously predictable outcome when lifeless chemicals interacted. Life had emerged from non-living atoms, and no degree of study of lifeless chemistry would make one an expert on the emergent property of life. The special level of organization of living organisms transcends the simpler organization of lifeless chemistry.

In *The Sacred Depths of Nature*, Ursula Goodenough describes such emergence as "Something more from nothing but." [69] From "nothing but" non-living chemicals, living organisms formed. This does not make the study of chemistry false or deny the necessity of non-living chemicals and their interactions to form living bodies. Yet the leap in complexity of organization of those same atoms when they become part of living organisms is definitely a stunning "Something more from nothing but."

Goodenough uses the analogy of a Mozart piano sonata to describe emergence. The whole, a beautiful piece of music, is the sum of parts organized at multiple levels. Mozart conceived the melody, transformed it into written notes ("... black specks on white paper ...") [70] from which an intermediate level of organization occurred, consisting of "chords and phrases and tempos and melodies...." [71] These organizational elements require translation by a piano through which a musician places pressure on a key, causing a hammer to strike a string, leading to the emergence of the whole, the audible and beautiful sonata, from the various levels at which its parts are organized.

Each level of organization in the Mozart sonata analogy contains its own truth, and each level up and down the chain of complexity affects the organization of the other levels. Mozart's abstract thought resulted in written nomenclature that encoded melodies that were transcribed by hammers and strings on a physical piano to send sound vibrations into the ears of listeners. In composing the notes and chords that make up the lower level of organization of the piece, Mozart was constrained by the physical structure and sound of the piano, the nature of the human ear, and the sense of beauty in the mind of both the composer and his listeners.

We see multiple levels of emergence when we consider the development of complex multicellular organisms from the one-celled organisms that are thought to be Earth's first living things. There is a code in each cell's DNA that translates some cells into eyes, some into heart or brain. Each requires unique complex chemistry and physical order to be part of an organ that is part of a system of organs that interacts with other organ systems to be part of a body. For example, brain cells have an internal chemistry that supports electrical connections to other brain cells, with chemical transmitters carrying messages between cells, all of which are organized anatomically, and have input and output channels to the rest of the nervous system and all its outposts throughout the body. The nervous system requires nutrients absorbed from the digestive system, oxygen from the respiratory system, circulation from the cardiovascular system, and so on. All these systems are themselves composed of subsystems, and all are integrated into the whole functioning body. At the base of the pyramid are the once-lifeless chemicals that have been organized into living components of a complex body, with multiple levels of organization creating subsystems of subsystems integrated into organs, which are themselves integrated into organ systems, whose interplay makes possible your life. There are levels of emergence within levels of emergence within levels of emergence.

You as a single organism do not represent the final level of emergence. You are part of multiple other systems. While you yourself are the result of the many levels of emergence that built your body and brought it to life, you are a single note integrated into multiple melodies that fill the universe. You are, as mentioned, part of a culture that has its own level of organization. You are a part of the human population of the world. You and all other organisms are part of local ecosystems, which are part of the planetary ecosystem. Each level of organization reflects the nature of its parts, but also creates relationships between its parts and thereby imposes order upon them. For example, ecosystems exist because various parts of a system offer other parts of the system the opportunity to survive. Energy, nutrients, and chemicals funnel back and forth between living and non-living parts of the ecosystem, dictated to some extent by the components of the system, but the system itself imposes constraints as well as opportunities.

Consider the one-celled bacterium E. coli. In fact, consider 10 billion of them. Previously lifeless atoms gather under the guidance of DNA to cross that amazing bridge from non-living to living, becoming E. coli. Yet not even a collection of 10 billion such bacteria would give any hint that consciousness or intelligence could develop in a collection of living cells. Consciousness is another emergent property of living beings, the surprising development of "Something more from nothing but."

At the base of your body's organizational structure, non-living matter entered your body and became alive, so part of what is happening is merely chemistry. Physically you are a collection of protons, neutrons, and electrons, plus various forms of energy. Most of the space both within and between atoms is felt to be empty. Take away the empty space and your protons, neutrons, and electrons would occupy *one billionth of a teaspoon.* [72] Add back the empty space, arrange the protons, neutrons, and electrons in just the right order, and amazingly there you are! Some of your ingredients were packaged into neurons, the specialized cells of the nervous system. Up and down the animal kingdom, various aggregations of neurons have formed brains capable of keeping organisms alive. There is controversy about how much intangible thought any given species might have, but one thing is for certain: say what you wish about the superiority of our own brain, but clearly the fox's brain knows what a fox must know to survive, as does a bat's or a butterfly's. Many animal behaviors are instinctive, pre-wired, but nonetheless brilliant in allowing that animal to live and procreate. Neurons singly may respond to simple stimuli such as whether an object is hot or cold or sharp - lower-level judgments. Yet combined in masses with the proper organization, such neurons within brains are capable of distinguishing dangers and opportunities, allowing each sentient species to choose successful strategies for ongoing life.

Consider your own brain. It weighs about 3 pounds. It has a physical existence and structure, and is not immune to physical laws. Made of chemicals, its function is dependent on chemistry. In operation, neurons employ electricity as well, so brain function is also subject to the laws of electricity. The attributes we typically associate with the human mind, such as abstract thought and reflection (including self-reflection), depend on these chemical and electrical events happening within the brain. "Mind" is an emergent property of the brain, yet another example of "Something more from nothing but." No amount of chemical or electrical knowledge will allow a scientist to understand how physical atoms in the brain generate intangible thought.

Technology is advancing so that brains can be scanned during certain types of thinking to localize which regions of the brain are active during a particular thought. On a functional MRI Scan, for example, different parts of the brain will light up if the person in the scanner is performing meditation or prayer or mathematical calculations. Certainly, electrochemical activity is taking place within localized regions of the brain concurrent with the process of thinking, and different modes of thinking are associated with different but reproducible patterns of brain activation. This demonstrates that a physical mechanism is involved in generating thought but still leaves us on the physical side of an unsolvable mystery. From a physical brain, abstract thought emerges, much of it deeply personal, through which we define ourselves and the world around us. The awareness of a single thought - this one - is as close as our own consciousness, and utterly beyond comprehension.

Our thoughts have been with us our entire life, and seem natural to us. We swim so often in mundane concerns, and rarely consider how remarkable it is that our physical bodies can experience such a rich mental life. To call "thought" or "self-reflection" an "emergent property of brain" does not solve its mystery. Yet we certainly must recognize how amazing it is that a 3-pound collection of cells can conjure up a mental universe. At any time, no matter what you are thinking, that thought is the product of an unknowable mechanism that leaps beyond the chemistry and electricity that we can understand.

To recognize through the process of self-awareness that you are capable of intangible thinking makes any such thought a passport to the World of Mystery. No trail of explanations leads across the bridge from one's current scientific knowledge to this inexplicable realm. You cannot understand how you have mentally reached such a land, but you can visit for as long as you like whenever you choose. Lifeless chemicals have been brought to life, and within the interacting systems and subsystems of your body, such chemicals casually generate consciousness and the intangible ideas that guide your life. How rare you must be in the universe to have such power!

Use that power now. Direct your thinking to realities worthy of your miraculous place in the universe. Look at a tree or a friend or your image in the mirror. Pay attention! Take the journey to the Land of the Inexplicable, the land of your own thoughts, that you have the power to visit this very moment. Wander its paths. Your physical body and 3-pound brain have equipped you for exploring this world of Mystery. Open your eyes, open your mind, be Yourself.

Rhythms

It is often said that we have five major senses - vision, hearing, touch, smell, and taste. Yet almost all organisms, with or without a wristwatch, possess an additional sense - they know how to tell time. The Earth they inhabit spins through space with a day-night cycle linked to its 24 hour rotation about its axis, with seasons dictated by its annual journey around the sun. Tides dance to the Moon's gravitational pull. Biologists Russell G. Foster and Leon Kreitzman point out that, "It is small wonder that the ability to anticipate and exploit these changes has an evolutionary advantage." The authors state, "We and just about every living thing on the planet - animals, plants, algae, bacteria — have a biological clock that was first set ticking more than three billion years ago." [73]

Daily rhythms such as sleep-wake cycles and eating patterns are superimposed on more long-term rhythms such as seasonally linked migration or reproductive patterns. The authors quote J. T. Fraser: "Animals and plants that share the same ecological niche must coordinate their biological rhythms; there must be a chasing time, an eating time, and drinking, mating and building times." [74]

Foster and Kreitzman point out the importance of plants and animals being able to anticipate sunrise and sunset to be "in the right state and in the right place at the right time." [75] For example, tobacco plants and evening primroses release scent near dusk to attract pollinating night-flying insects and moths. The production of scented oils must be appropriately timed and requires preparation. The daily cycle of the plants and the insects, plus the nocturnal predators such as bats and owls that emerge near sunset, represents an interwoven ecosystem in which an organism's internal sense of time is coordinated with the rhythms of other living things and the planet they inhabit.

In tidal zones, the Moon generates high and low tides twice daily, superimposed on the day-night cycle. Plants and animals, predators and prey, survive best if their internal rhythm is accurate. Intertidal rhythms of about 12.8 hours, reflecting the lunar gravitational pull, somehow influence organisms that would be dragged to sea or devoured if they popped out of the sand at the wrong time.

Cicadas live as nymphs underground for 13 or 17 years, before some timer within them triggers their molt into winged adults that emerge above ground, shed their exoskeletons, rattle out their courtship songs, and live 2 to 4 more weeks. During this brief, if noisy, aboveground sojourn, they mate and lay eggs in tree branches, where 6 to 10 weeks later, new nymphs are born. The nymphs fall to the ground, burrow 6 to 18 inches underground to feed, set their internal timer at 13 or 17 years, and the life cycle continues. The cues that trigger a cycle of 13 or 17 years must be perceived by the cicada underground, and no one has figured out how they count the years. The unusual cycle length might prevent them from acquiring any natural above-ground enemies, since their infrequent emergence might prove puzzling to the more regular denizens of an ecosystem.

On a more regular basis, successful reproductive strategies require having young at a time of year when food is available. Foster and Kreitzman state that most animals use day length to cue their mating practices. For birds and small mammals with short pregnancies, increasing day length in the spring or perhaps early summer triggers mating. Large mammals like sheep and deer, with gestation periods of 5-9 months, mate with an internal calendar based on decreasing day length in the autumn, with birth then occurring in spring or early summer.

How can an animal figure out if this is mating season? A key appears to be the timing of melatonin release by the pineal gland, which increases during the hours of night, and therefore serves as an internal representation of the day-night cycle. Long hours of melatonin release coincide with long hours of nighttime, which further coincides with winter. The specific day-night ratio therefore is a representation of a particular calendar date of the year. Equal day-night ratio represents the spring or autumn equinox, typically around March 20th and September 22nd, which also are important dates for timing seasonal migrations. Therefore the eye, by providing day-night information, is giving calendar information, as represented internally by melatonin secretion.

The so-called master clock in many animals resides in a cluster of cells in a part of the brain called the suprachiasmatic nuclei, located in the anterior hypothalamus. In mammals, this cluster consists of about 20,000 cells. It is the suprachiasmatic nuclei that stimulate melatonin output from the pineal, which in a normal cycle rises about two hours before expected sleep, but which is daily recalibrated to the observed day-night cycle. Day length is the primary external cue that results in an interaction between the hypothalamic suprachiasmatic nuclei and pineal melatonin release, all resulting in a cascade of sexual chemical release for seasonally mating animals when the proper day-night ratio arrives. Thus the hypothalamus-pineal-melatonin system, in addition to modulating an animal's sleep cycle, also serves as a calendar that informs the animal whether it is time to mate or migrate.

Our own species, still deeply embedded in sleep-wake cycles linked to the day-night cycle, no longer times its reproduction to the seasons. We do try to fool other species to time their reproduction to cycles chosen by us. Racehorses race as one, two, or three-year-olds based on their age January 1st. Breeders want potential racehorses to be born early in a new year, so that they can be the most physically mature members of their age bracket. In the wild, mares conceive in the late spring or early summer and give birth 11 months later in late spring. Breeders alter this pattern by keeping mares in stalls with bright lighting through the night to mimic longer days that induce the mares to conceive earlier and give birth in January or February of the following year. [76]

Cows are exposed to prolonged natural lighting to improve their milk production by 8-10%, and tulip growers use red artificial light at night to induce year-round flowering. [77] We have learned what cues other life forms use to trigger their natural processes, and modified their behavior by modifying their cues.

Other key survival patterns for most organisms depend on successful responses to seasonal changes. Many species in nature have certain seasons that are optimal for them, and other seasons that they must survive and endure. Being able to anticipate when bitter cold will arrive, when food will become unavailable, also requires a sense of time for appropriate preparation and action.

The winter world looks so radically different from the summer world, yet each enduring species has developed methods for successfully navigating both. An early freeze can kill unprepared trees, though a deeper freeze later in winter can be well tolerated by a similar tree after it has had time to make seasonal adaptations to cold. Deciduous trees begin dropping their leaves and cutting back to minimal basic core metabolic processes as day length shortens in the autumn, and as temperatures start downward, so that fewer vulnerable metabolic processes are exposed to winter freezes. I have often seen Texas trees begin dropping their leaves in September or October, when the thermometer still reads 90-100 degrees, but signals such as shrinking day length tell them it is time to begin winterizing. Grass spends winters dormant till the warmer weather of spring reignites photosynthesis for a new year.

Migrating species require preparation before enacting travel plans. The fur of many mammals thickens as winter approaches; birds time their molts to coordinate with their travel and mating schedule. These are not spur-of-the-moment decisions. While winters or summers at most locales will vary at least somewhat from year to year, and can therefore be an unreliable indicator of seasonal information, day length in the middle latitudes is a steady guide to calendar date. A particular day-night ratio occurs for example one day each spring and one day each autumn, and migrating species are paying careful attention. (Of course, day length is not a useful guide in polar regions, where the sun never falls below the horizon for months each summer or rises above it for months each winter, and equatorial areas, where days and nights remain equal throughout the year.)

Animals appear to use the suprachiasmatic nuclei-pineal gland-melatonin system to convert visual information about day length into a calendar sense to guide winter strategies such as migration. To take it a step further, visual information about length of daylight seems to activate genes in key tissues such as the suprachiasmatic nuclei, and the expression of these different genetic patterns translates into behavioral changes.

We of the species Homo sapiens are strange interlopers against the backdrop of living organisms whose rhythms are so intimately woven into the rhythms of Earth. Since our invention of clock time, we in many ways dissociate ourselves from the rhythms of nature. Still, the diurnal rhythm that drives nocturnal sleep is deeply ingrained, though many modern jobs require work at times that are not physiologically optimal.

Foster and Kreitzman report studies that suggest humans living in experimental locations with no day-night cues cycle through daily rhythms over an average cycle of 24 hours and 11 minutes. Outside experimental settings, we use external cues (such as an alarm clock or sunrise) to synchronize ourselves daily to the 24-hour schedule of our culture. Other than the usual pattern of sleeping at night, it is remarkable the extent to which we deny the existence of internal rhythms. We certainly no longer use seasonal or day length cues to regulate mating behavior, developing a sex drive that is unrelated to seasonal cycles.

We chop the day into 24 equal hours of 60 equal minutes containing 60 equal seconds, and link our own schedule during these artificially created intervals with the schedules of others. This optimizes a certain kind of efficiency, while preventing us from responding to our own internal rhythms. We eat our meals, not in response to physiologic hunger, but at pre-scheduled mealtimes. Our sleep ends, not when we are rested and have naturally awakened, but when the alarm sounds. Just as artificial lighting is used to improve the yield of tulips or milk cows, we use nocturnal artificial lighting in an attempt to increase our own productivity.

Our body temperature tends to be lower in the morning and increase by one-half to one degree Fahrenheit over the course of the day. Athletic performance such as swimming speed seems to follow a similar trajectory. Intellectual capabilities on average tend to be relatively lower overnight, improving by late morning and early afternoon. Asthma flare-ups tend to disproportionately occur late in the day. [78] To our bodies, those time intervals that our culture treats as interchangeable are not equivalent.

We have generally accepted a pattern of life increasingly out of touch with our own internal biological nature. An indoor environment shields us from much of the impact of seasonal change, and we determine our next activity by consulting a clock rather than our own internal inclination.

As you think about your own life, is there a way you can reclaim some freedom to respond to the wisdom of your own body, with all its sensors to keep you informed of its state and its intrinsic needs? As you observe the living things in the world around you, consider how different forms of life sew themselves into the fabric of daytime and nighttime, into summer and winter. Think of all the changes they must successfully make for their species to continue. Each oak tree or beetle or chickadee has a survival saga to relate, partly thanks to its ability to tell time and date.

Flashlight

A flashlight can be considered a device for seeking truth. When you are surrounded by darkness, a flashlight can make truth visible in the area illuminated. Yet when environmentalist and former park ranger Edward Abbey in *Desert Solitaire* walked through the desert at night, his preference was to leave his flashlight turned off. In this way, he was able to dimly perceive many features of a broad landscape. When he turned the flashlight on, a small circle in the path of the beam was brightly illuminated, but this focal bright light made the rest of the landscape outside the beam disappear into blackness. [79] The flashlight, in allowing Abbey to learn a lot about a little, erased his ability to dimly perceive the environment in which his localized truth was embedded.

The sun performs the same trick. The sun not only shines light that allows us to visualize the true features of our planet, but it also limits our vision in other ways. We certainly see the world in crisp detail during daylight and stumble in night's darkness. Yet like Abbey's flashlight, the sun both reveals and conceals. In daytime, sunlight generates a certain perspective of reality, a local comforting perspective that displays in detail the trees, automobiles, and buildings of the planet we inhabit and feel we know. We get the impression viewing the world by sunlight that our planetary reality *is* reality.

After sunset, when the flashlight of the sun on our planet has been turned off, we see in the dark night sky deep space, where stars and galaxies give notice of a larger universe in which our planet and sun are immersed. This larger truth lies hidden all around us throughout the day, but sunlight blinds us to its existence. One truth conceals another. Daytime sunlight shines on us and our activities, casting a spotlight on us at center stage. Nighttime and starlight remind us that the relative certainties we experience at noon are embedded in an immense universe of deep mystery.

Each way of looking at reality is another flashlight. Each flashlight can provide a window into Truth but can blind us to other realities that exist outside its beam. Our vision is partly blinded by what we see, our knowledge by what we know, our hopes for deeper understanding by what we currently understand. Through our limits we must perceive the limitless. Through the small circle illuminated by our flashlight, we must sense the infinite mystery that places the light in our hands and gives us the power to search.

Infinity

There is a lot of Universe out there, a lot of Mystery. Our Earth gives us an annual chariot ride around the Sun through a comfortable and familiar astronomical neighborhood. However, any news we receive from other stars is based on energy they radiated or deflected toward our planet at some time in the past, like postcards written in code long ago from exotic lands we can never visit. It may take light hundreds, thousands, millions, or billions of years to reach us from distant stars, and from this potentially ancient information we conceptualize the possible structure and evolution of the universe. Our Sun is one of at least 100 billion stars in the Milky Way Galaxy; the Milky Way itself is one of about 100 billion galaxies in the observable universe, and all the galaxies but a small part of our own are unreachable by our species. Almost everything that exists is Terra Incognita on our map of the universe.

While we know general theories of star formation and structure and therefore generalities about star systems, essentially everything that exists in the universe lies beyond our reach. Jeffrey Bennett, Seth Shostak, and Bruce Jakosky estimate that the number of stars in the universe is approximately equal to the number of grains of sand of all the beaches on Earth added together, so it is as if we are trying to deduce Ultimate Truth while gravitationally bound to the third planet orbiting one of those sand grains. [80]

Even that analogy understates the difficulty of understanding our true relationship to the universe. Joel R. Primack and Nancy Ellen Abrams point out that the entire visible universe constitutes about one-half of one percent of the total universe. Atoms of so-called ordinary matter, of which we are composed, make up about 5% of the universe. That leaves 95% of the universe not only unexplainable, but made of different stuff than we are. Current scientific theory calls this stuff "dark matter" and "dark energy," dark to our comprehension as well as our eyes. [81] Here we ride on a planet orbiting a proverbial grain of sand in a universe almost entirely composed of dark matter and dark energy, which we have been unable to identify or access. How much Ultimate Truth are we capable of grasping when it is shielded from us by impenetrable layers of mystery? It is difficult enough trying to remember what we had for lunch.

You might think time would be on our side, presuming that the rapid advance of science could eventually open the curtain that conceals the deepest processes of the universe. Yet the universe seems to be expanding at an accelerating rate, so that galaxies that are not gravitationally bound to each other appear to be flying away from us faster and faster, carrying vital evidence with them. Such a rapidly expanding universe would likely come to a quiet and lonely ending, as scattered stars burn out like embers floating from a fading campfire, though there may be innumerable other universes, some of which could be young and vibrant when ours fades.

If this scenario turns out to be true, we are granted only a brief peek at our universe. As astrophysicist (and one time pop musician) Brian Cox and BBC Science writer Andrew Cohen put it in *Wonders of The Universe*, "As a fraction of the lifespan of the Universe, as measured from its beginning to the evaporation of the last black hole, life as we know it is only possible for one-thousandth of a billion billion billionth, billion billion billionth, billion billion billionth of a per cent." [82]

They continue, "And that's why, for me, the most astonishing wonder of the Universe isn't a star or a planet or a galaxy; it isn't a thing at all - it's a moment in time. And that time is now." [83]

The Mystery Problem is complicated by the Infinity Problem. We cannot grasp numbers or spaces that continue without end.

Does the universe go on forever? If not, is anything outside it? If the universe had a beginning, did Nothing exist before that, and did that Nothing exist forever? Is the universe part of something larger that does or does not go on forever? Our minds were not built for wrestling with eternities or infinities.

It does not even take something big to house infinity. Between the numbers zero and one, there are an infinite number of fractions. Pick any number, no matter how high, and the space between zero and one can be divided into that many parts. In fact, pick any two decimal fractional numbers such as .000001 (with 5 zeros) and .0000001 (with 6 zeros), and there exist an infinite number of decimal fractional numbers between them. To find an infinite collection of numbers, we do not have to look to the infinitely large, but only to look more closely at the apparently small space between any two numbers. Infinities lie within infinities.

With so much deep mystery and so many infinities all around us, are the truths we are able to access doomed to be small, small enough that our 3-pound brain can comprehend them? Certainly our brains are very good at solving many types of local problems; they excel at survival skills. You are unlikely to run into a task today that your skull-enclosed brain does not have the talent to address, though mysteries float around the periphery of awareness. When we run into a process of great complexity, a common approach is to create a simpler model that is understandable. Complex processes such as the vagaries of the world economy are reduced to simplified models that can be processed by computers to make predictions and plans. Obviously such a strategy is no better than its model, and the infinitely complex is not easily modeled.

Trying to comprehend the incomprehensible sometimes involves the two-edged sword of language. When a comprehensible word is used to describe a Great Mystery, something of importance can be lost. The concept of the Infinite cannot be mentally condensed to a size small enough that words can hold it. Beware the conceit that the Infinite can be held in properly punctuated sentences or even understood. Be tolerant when others, likewise struggling to comprehend Mystery, use different words than you to describe their quest.

Almost all numbers are fractions, lying between the whole numbers like one and two and three by which we count. Almost all sounds are at vibrational frequencies that lie between the notes that make up the standardized scales of our music. Words and numbers and notes skim the surface of the Infinite.

One strategy to navigate through a world of mystery is to pick a small enough human-sized mystery to explore. When I attended medical school, I was introduced to one of my professors as follows: "This is Dr._____. He will teach you everything you ever wanted to know about toad bladders." At the time, I thought the professor had chosen a strange direction in his search to unravel the mysteries of the universe, yet I suppose it is as good a choice as any. The survival of living organisms depends on assimilating the molecules necessary for survival and expelling the rest, so I suppose if one learns enough about toad bladders, one gains a key toward understanding the puzzle of life. Mysteries wrapped in mysteries - tiny Rosetta stone toad bladders allowing the existence of larger mysteries called toads, drawing life from a planet within a galaxy within a universe. With all this swirling around us, we - like my professor - must live out our lives at our human scale.

Best known for his travel writing, William Least Heat-Moon in *Blue Highways* visits an East Texas mound that 1,000 years ago was the center of a Caddo Indian village and now has been taken over by blackberry bushes. He states, "The aura of time the mound gave off seemed to mock any comprehension of its change and process - how it had grown from baskets of shoveled soil to the high center of Caddoan affairs to a hilly patch of blackberries. My rambling metaphysics was getting caught in the trap of reducing experience to coherence and meaning, letting the perplexity of things disrupt the joy in their mystery. To insist that diligent thought would bring an understanding of change was to limit life to the comprehensible." [84]

How guilty are we of "limiting life to the comprehensible"? Life becomes small if we reduce it to small terms, sweeping from our daily experience a sense of wonder. Is our life a trudge from task to task? Why not a journey from incomprehensible miracle to incomprehensible miracle? We know how to drive to work and what to do there. Most jobs require logical, finite thinking, but this does not make the infinite features of the universe disappear. Yet looking at the world only through our understanding is like viewing it with a different type of flashlight, one that illuminates what we can intellectually comprehend while blinding us to what lies outside its circle of visibility. The flashlight of rationality is useful for many important tasks, and we would certainly be lost without it. Knowledge and comprehension are obviously essential to survival. Yet be cautious of "limiting life to the comprehensible" - what one searches for limits what one finds. Though man may be unique compared to other animals in his aptitude for logic and reason, he is surely equally unique in his ability to see beyond logic and reason.

Gaze at any living thing, and consider how little of it is understandable. Once you know how to identify a bird by the pattern of its feathers or its song, and have learned what it eats, how much about that bird do you really know? What thoughts or instincts drive its behavior? What in turn drives those thoughts and instincts? In nature, a sequence of answerable questions often traces back to unanswerable ones.

When we interact with each other, we tend to reduce the indecipherable mystery that you are and I am to create simplistic models of each other. Perhaps I know whether you like to play golf or go to the movies, what you enjoy talking about. We exchange understandable words in proper linguistic sequence. We say "Hi," when we pass each other. Yet we remain great mysteries even to ourselves. Within us, private joys and sorrows bubble, passions erupt for no apparent reason, inexplicable. We talk with words, leaving much unspoken, sometimes revealing more in a brief glance or gesture than in a stream of language with proper syntax. Flashlights hide a great deal outside their beam.

I do not know how I develop a single thought, or how you do. I think of our universe as a place packed with incomprehensible infinities. Within it, small islands of understanding develop within oceans of mystery. Yet what are these islands of understanding?

To understand anything, to grasp truth and neurologically encode it with a brain, is itself miraculous.

It may seem life is a daily sequence - easily captured by words - of breakfast, work, dinner, television, sleep, then repeat. Guy Murchie shifts the focus from the tangible to the mysterious in this two-sentence history of the universe: "But gradually radiation evolved matter and matter evolved worlds and worlds turned out to be alive, self-sufficient and full of mystic potentiality. By self-sufficient I mean that life (including human life) eats, drinks and breathes the earth - and also the sun and the Milky Way and the universe." [85]

You are like the infinite set of fractions between zero and one, an interwoven set of miracles. Through the many moments of your life, you are given the privilege of dancing with Infinity, which is disguised in many forms. The process cannot be understood, but the Universe invites you to dance as its partner.

Roller Coaster

It is impossible to merely stand pat in this life. Even if you try to stay in the same place, time and the planet Earth move onward. Dr. Michael Wysession explains how the planet on which you are standing is guaranteed to take you on a ride no midway could match. [86]

For example, between the time you awoke yesterday morning and the time you awoke today, Earth gave you one revolution around its axis. If your bed was at the equator, you traveled the Earth's circumference of 25,000 miles or 40,000 kilometers in that single spin. If you live in the middle latitudes, you traveled half as far.

Your chariot, the Earth, was moving around the sun at about 30 kilometers per second, approximately 100,000 kilometers (over 60,000 miles) per hour, so you have ventured almost two and a half million kilometers (almost one and a half million miles) around the sun between yesterday's awakening and today's. Each second, the sun journeys 220 kilometers around the center of the Milky Way

Galaxy, and transports you some 19 million kilometers (almost 12 million miles) over that 24 hours.

If you started reading this section about 15 seconds ago, the Milky Way Galaxy has itself traveled over 8,000 kilometers (over 5,000 miles) during that time relative to surrounding galaxies, as it orbits the center of the universe at a velocity of about 550 kilometers or 340 miles per second. It is unknown if the universe is part of a larger structure, a "multiverse," so we cannot know if our universe itself is moving relative to something else.

The universe certainly seems to be expanding, with much debate about the rate of expansion and the degree to which this adds to the cosmic voyage you have taken since you awoke yesterday morning. Unquestionably, you have traveled millions and millions of miles over the course of one single day – each day, every day.

You are not alone on your journey. Billions of other people, countless blades of grass, hosts of insects and bacteria and tuna fish traveled with you through otherwise lifeless realms of space. Almost all your fellow travelers think they are more or less in the same place that they were yesterday, doing the same activities and facing the same routine, but you know better. You have the wisdom to recognize that we are cosmic travelers, effortlessly soaring millions of miles. Most of those who travel with you are blind to their journey, while you have the awareness each night to watch planets and galaxies drift by.

There is no standing still in this life. Tomorrow you will be millions of miles away, with new adventures waiting. You don't even need a spacesuit, since the Earth will feed and support you while serving as your spaceship. Don't even try to cling like a barnacle to a single spot. Open your imagination, and let us meet again many millions of miles from here tomorrow.

"Cosmic Shooting Gallery"

Of course, all that interstellar travel comes with a certain degree of risk. In *Earth: The Biography*, Iain Stewart and John Lynch point out some of the hazards: "We live on a rock-coated metal ball hurtling at 66,000 mph (107,000km/h) through space. It's an unsettling thought not made any less so by the knowledge that the space we're careering through is far from empty. Like a car speeding through congested city streets, our breakneck orbit around the sun takes us across the path of millions of projectiles - everything from tiny pebbles to rocks the size of the Ukraine." [87]

The very process of building our planet required uncountable collisions of rocks floating in space that were drawn into each other and held together by gravity, forming larger and larger structures that collided and stuck together until reaching planetary size. Essentially all the planets and moons of our solar system have borne the brunt of collisions with other astronomical objects such as comets and asteroids. Stewart and Lynch state, "… it doesn't take much to appreciate that we live in a cosmic shooting gallery." [88] Each crater on the Moon is evidence of an impact where some astronomical object crash-landed, and the early Earth is close enough to the Moon that it must have undergone a similar bombardment.

It is thought that the Moon itself was formed from a collision between the Earth and a smaller planet whose orbit intersected ours in the early history of our solar system. The other planet, retrospectively named Theia, is speculated to have smashed into Earth about 4.4 billion years ago. The outer crustal material from both planets was blown out into space and condensed into our Moon, while the cores of the two planets merged, with Earth's core growing by 20% in the merger. [89] This increased mass led to an increase in Earth's gravity, so that it could develop and hold an atmosphere, which helped burn up many future meteors by friction before they could reach the planet's surface. Gases within the atmosphere eventually were inhaled by living organisms on Earth, and modified by those organisms in a process that continues to this day. We ourselves breathe and modify the atmosphere.

Hence the Moon contains atoms that once were part of Earth and of Theia, and it is slowly moving away from us as its orbit carries it outward. Shortly after its formation, the Moon was close enough that it would have appeared 10 times bigger to an earthly viewer, of which at that time there were none. [90] The Moon and Earth mutually orbit their common center of gravity (which lies within the Earth), stabilizing Earth's orbit in relation to the Sun. Prior to that time, Earth wobbled irregularly under the gravitational influence of other planets in our solar system, which would have resulted in wild swings in temperature and tidal forces. Once the Earth and Moon became dance partners, this new stability reduced tidal and temperature extremes, paving the way for the eventual development of life on our planet. We have survived ice ages, and it has been a long time since Earth boiled during the course of its cosmic travels. Our relationship with the Moon deserves some credit for that stability.

In the early era of the Earth-Moon relationship, Earth days were thought to be about five hours long. Gradually Earth's spin is slowing, with longer days of 24 hours, as its companion drifts farther away at a rate of about one and a half inches per year. There certainly continue to be meteor impacts, such as the one that is thought to have doomed the dinosaurs and paved the way for the spread of mammals. Astronomers are hard at work identifying and tracking potential meteors that might be a planetary threat, and plenty of rocks of varying sizes and orbits are floating around. Jupiter has been a good and well-positioned big brother, screening away many potential meteors with its powerful gravity, and holding in its gravitational embrace a belt of asteroids that might otherwise stray our direction. Every night, small pebble-size rocks from space enter our atmosphere and burn up; most never reach the ground.

There is a high likelihood that rocks from space may have borne special gifts. Currently, living organisms possess the remarkable capability of reproduction, but it remains uncertain where the original raw materials to start the process came from. We have a chicken versus egg conundrum: today's DNA requires protein to copy itself, but today's proteins require DNA for their synthesis. How did Earth acquire the first of either to initiate the process?

Amino acids, the building blocks of proteins, have been found on meteorites after epic journeys through space. Likewise, some combinations of atoms found in present-day DNA and RNA have ridden to Earth on meteors. It is not known to what extent, if any, these served as precursors to the development of our planet's DNA and proteins. The possibility exists that such molecules may have played an important role in the development of earthly life.

As we count our blessings, we must think about Earth's charmed travels through the universe, taking a hit from time to time while acquiring meteor-borne organic molecules, gaining a moon in the process, but maintaining conditions that have sustained life for billions of years. It is interesting on a clear dark night to watch "shooting stars" trail across the sky; each is a rock that has traveled across unfathomable distances of space to burn up in our atmosphere. During meteor showers, Earth is traveling through clusters of such rocks that sparkle as they burn through the darkness.

Look at the Moon with its craters. Through the "cosmic shooting gallery" we fly.

BACKYARD MEDITATIONS

Look deeply, I arrive in every second
To be a bud on a spring branch,
To be a tiny bird, with wings still fragile,
Learning to sing in my new nest ...

Thich Nhat Hanh

Sitting silently,
Doing nothing,
Spring comes,
And the grass grows by itself.

Basho

All know that the drop merges into the ocean, but few know that
the ocean merges into the drop.

Kabir

... we cannot understand a stone without some understanding of
the great sun.

Maria Montessori
To Educate the Human Potential

Meditations

I must plead guilty to walking unawares past some very remarkable things. It could be said that I often lacked "mindfulness." For example, I could look up the 1968 population of Brazil on a computer in my house without considering the amazing process through which the vast power of computer networks is accessible to me. I could watch a sporting event happening right now thousands of miles away on a television in my living room, and pay attention to the actions of the athletes, without giving a moment's thought to the technological brilliance through which those images appear on my screen. Like most people, I would perceive the display - the information on the computer screen, the televised show - without thinking about the process through which the technology works.

These are examples of human ingenuity in which the newest model soon becomes outdated, while the latest advances follow in quick succession. Each reminds me what a clever species we are, but also how easily we take for granted technology that would have been unimaginable to the wealthiest rulers in prior human eras.

Throughout history, there have been attempts at maximizing the gift of life. Some cultures and individuals glorify achievement, trying to win as many of life's battles as possible. Conversely, mystics of many different traditions seek deeper truths by secluding themselves from those battles. Yet, other life possibilities exist besides the cloister or the battleground of contentious society.

There are many paths to Awareness. One could camp in a desert, go on a fast, or attend a retreat, all of which are methods to escape the mundane problems that beset our daily routines. One could meditate on one's breathing, or on a mantra, a sound or word or phrase that is repeated silently, as a means of focusing consciousness. Seeking awareness through any of these modes of escape from the everyday world implies that "ordinary" life is our trap, and Truth is to be found elsewhere. We must spend most of our precious hours within this ordinary life. Surely here we can find meaningful meditations.

Given that we are surrounded by wonders, both natural and technological, we have ample opportunity to perceive the extraordinary in the ordinary. It is there now. To discover it, we need only heighten our awareness of the remarkable processes manifested in commonplace forms. The inner workings of a tree take place under cover of a nondescript gray bark; the timeless cloaks itself in the temporal. Technology is dazzling, but its rapid advance leaves me without any handholds that would not soon be obsolete. Should technology be your fascination, by all means let it fascinate you. Let it be your access to a heightened appreciation of being You.

For me personally, the forms of nature hold special meaning. Many such forms have persisted essentially unchanged for thousands (or millions!) of years through processes of continual renewal. There I find my meditations, my ticket into the beauty that is everyday life. I seek not to seclude myself from ordinary life, but to dive into it.

William Bryant Logan in *Dirt* asks the simple question, "Why is Earth's dirt special?" Why, surrounded by so many lifeless stars, do we have a planetary skin from which millions of species take life? Logan responds to his own question, "... that we don't, and possibly can't, know the answer.... What's more, it seems that things that can't be figured out can still be *seen* to be true." Among his recommendations is "... meditation, not on some mantra but on the created.... [91]

Here then are some of my meditations, my attempts at mindfulness, developed in my backyard and during a weekend at the beach. It begins by walking out my back door and asking, "How do the most ordinary things happen?"

Trees

Author and "Beat Poet" Gary Snyder relates that indigenous populations throughout history thought of the Earth as alive and "learned what particular kinds of plants the ground would 'say' at that spot." [92] A tree can be considered what the cosmic process "speaking" through Earth has generated in a spot as accessible as my backyard.

I was inspired in my thinking about trees by Guy Murchie's *The Seven Mysteries of Life*, and borrow heavily from his ideas, which I first read decades ago. He introduces the topic by saying that, "... vegetation in quite a real sense does bind the sky to the Earth. Not only is vegetation the land's chief organ for absorbing rain that falls from the clouds and (after using it briefly) evaporating the same rain from its leaves back into the sky to maintain the terrestrial circulation, but vegetation quickens and conserves the entire atmosphere by inhaling excess carbon dioxide and exhaling vital oxygen, the while holding up mountain ranges, stemming erosion with stems, rooting soil with roots, directing the courses of brooks and rivers and literally leashing stationary clouds to wooded slopes with invisible thongs of humid wind." [93]

Start with contemplating the interaction between a tree's roots and the planet. "But the tiny root cap (its advancing tip) is only the first of several specialized parts which, working together, enable the root to steer its zigzag or spiral course, skirting serious obstacles, compromising with offensive substances, judiciously groping for grips on the more congenial rocks, secreting powerful acids to dissolve the uncongenial ones, heading generally downward in search of moisture and minerals while ever careful not to run completely out of air." [94] Via its roots a tree can form favorable alliances with other organisms, such as "when their roots go exploring, almost calling, through the ground for vital minerals, an act that provokes the ground in return to arise and answer the roots in the form of invisible threads of fungus containing those very minerals...." [95] The fungi are very effective in their wide-ranging abilities to digest substances within their reach, but benefit from the alliance with trees by receiving from the roots energy that the tree has captured via photosynthesis. The exchange of chemicals and water between tree and planet is further enhanced by root hairs that enormously increase the surface area of a tree's root system. Through its roots, trees and other plants "... steadily stitch themselves into the earth." [96]

It is also through its roots that a tree drinks water evaporated from distant oceans, which has floated through the atmosphere, congregated into drops too heavy to be borne further by its magic carpet of air, and fallen earthward as rain. Water unfurls leaves and points each blade of grass skyward. The chemical reactions that support a tree's life require the presence of water both as a participant and as a transport agent to move the other chemicals around, giving the tree on multiple scales a circulatory system. "The tree thus drinks in the manner of a very water-dependent beast, its total thirst actually far exceeding that of any animal on Earth." [97]

If it is the job of the roots to mine from the Earth the planetary chemicals that are brought to life within the tree, it is the commonplace nature of leaves to incorporate air, and add to the recipe sunlight absorbed after a 93 million mile journey through space. A leaf, again quoting Murchie, is "… not only a breathing organ but a bustling, automatic food factory full of tubes, retorts, chambers, valves and shutters operated by more timers, thermostats, hygrostats, feedback and catalytic controls (some of conflicting or unknown motivation) than anyone has yet been able to assess." [98] Pores, mostly on the underside of a leaf, regulate the flow of water and gases in and out of the photosynthetic assembly. Within the leaves of green plants, energy from sunlight is trapped by the chlorophyll molecule. For the tiniest fraction of a second, the chlorophyll molecule is driven into a higher energy state by the absorbed light, and via a complex network of reactants and catalysts, this energy is utilized in each leaf to synthesize carbohydrates (complex sugar molecules). This is the process of photosynthesis, the conversion of solar energy to the chemical energy within carbohydrates that powers most life on Earth.

These carbohydrates not only provide energy for the plant, but also for any animal that eats the plant, and on up the food chain to any animals that eat that animal. The energy we receive when we eat a meal represents a transfer to us of energy from prior sunlight. In photosynthesis, water molecules are split into hydrogen and oxygen. The hydrogen is combined with carbon dioxide to synthesize the carbohydrates, while oxygen is released into the air, to be inhaled by us.

It is this process of photosynthesis occurring in every leaf of every tree and plant that turns the energy from a star into the energy that supports life on our planet. The life-sustaining oxygen we draw into our lungs has been invisibly exhaled into the atmosphere through the eons by leaves.

The transport of chemicals up from the roots and down from the leaves requires a circulation network within the tree, which is called xylem. The veins within leaves represent the upper terminus of pathways that extend through the trunk down into the roots. Within the trunk, hidden inside the bland outer covering of bark, a network of tubes transports water with its associated chemicals (sap) throughout the living organism. As water evaporates from the leaves, a sort of negative pressure is created there that draws water upward through the tubing all the way from the roots. As water flows up and down, it carries minerals and nutrients to the living cells.

In the words of Annie Dillard: "There's a real power here. It is amazing that trees can turn gravel and bitter salts into these soft-lipped lobes, as if I were to bite down on a granite slab and start to swell, bud, and flower. Trees seem to do their feats so effortlessly. Every year a given tree creates absolutely from scratch ninety-nine percent of its living parts. Water lifting up tree trunks can climb one hundred and fifty feet an hour; in full summer a tree can, and does, heave a ton of water every day. A big elm in a single season might make as many as six million leaves, wholly intricate, without budging an inch...." [99]

All the complex parts of the tree, with its ability to bring life to earth and air, arose from a seed. Quoting Murchie, the seed ... "possesses a world-changing power that is truly mystic in the sense that it can potentially reproduce not only the complete tree or plant it came from, but all the trees that can descend from that one, indeed (if conditions are favorable) whole forests of them...." [100] Two 2,000-year-old lotus seeds discovered in Japan in 1951 were planted and flowered normally, as did frozen 10,000-year-old lupine seeds found in the Yukon tundra. One champion specimen is a single aspen tree in Utah with 47,000 trunks sharing a single root system and existing as a single plant. [101]

So successful is the tree as a lifestyle that they make up most of the weight of all multicellular organisms on Earth. According to British professor, John D. Barrow, mathematician and physicist, plants make up 97.3% of the weight of Earth's multicellular organisms, and the great majority of that weight is found in trees. [102] By comparison, the human race makes up 0.01% of the biosphere by weight. How does any of this happen? The survival of some seeds for thousands of years is only a minor footnote in the story of trees. Without any real-life "Methuselan" seeds, the tree saga would be just as remarkable. It is one of the countless interwoven melodies our universe plays. Each tree stands before us, inviting us to meditate on its interconnections and to let our mind engage the mystery within its leaves and bark. Caught up in a man-made vortex of commodity prices, politics, international intrigue, and the struggles of the local sports franchise, we can feel like tiny pawns in an unstable human network. Each tree offers a door out of this psychological trap and into the Miraculous, a door that can be opened Here and Now.

Butterflies

Every living thing offers proof that the miracle of its existence has happened. Butterflies, so common, so lovely and fragile, have quite a story to tell. Butterflies share with moths the biological order called Lepidoptera, containing over 165,000 species, of which 90% are moths. It is perhaps because moths are more active at night, when fewer predators are around, that they hold such a numerical advantage. There are many metamorphoses in the lifestyle of these organisms, in which the same "stuff" gets re-arranged into completely different forms through the course of a lifetime.

The story begins with a fertilized egg deposited by the mother butterfly or moth who must possess a certain knowledge of botany. She must identify a plant that her caterpillar offspring will be able to eat, and some species always pick the same plant. She also needs to make locational choices, seeking a spot either underneath a leaf and thereby out of sight to potential predators, or at least camouflaged. Every phase of the butterfly's life is perilous in a world in which small, slow-moving life forms often become quick meals.

After breaking open the egg, out crawls the caterpillar, like a complex worm on legs. The caterpillar starts crawling around eating its host plant, multiplying in size over a thousand-fold, typically within weeks. Its fulltime job is eating. This creates a new problem, one faced by human children who outgrow their clothes. The caterpillar solves the problem of how to cover itself by molting perhaps four times, dissolving or shaking loose from its tight-fitting outer lining to grow a bigger one. The part of the lining that is dissolved can be promptly recycled, as its ingredients are incorporated into the caterpillar's fast-growing body. After each molt, the caterpillar may have a completely different appearance that can puzzle predators. If it is foul-tasting or toxic, the caterpillar advertises this with glaring colors in its lining.

If caterpillars develop immunity to a plant toxin, they will eat the toxin to make themselves distasteful or poisonous to potential predators, and again advertise their toxicity with bright coloring that other species will mimic. Otherwise they often seek safety in camouflage, matching their color to that of their host plant. Caterpillars also can have multiple spines like small swords sticking out from their bodies to discourage predators.

Then comes the act of prestidigitation for which butterflies and moths are famous. After choosing a location it hopes will be undiscovered, the caterpillar begins secreting a silk cocoon. The ancient Chinese thousands of years ago developed a system of growing a breed of moth caterpillar called a "silkworm" on mulberry leaves, and then harvesting and unwinding the cocoons to obtain precious silk. The strand from a single cocoon would typically be 600 to 900 meters long (900 meters is about 1,000 yards, over half a mile of silk). Still today, the caterpillar within its self-made silk cocoon undergoes its final molt. Some species perform this metamorphosis entirely enclosed behind the curtain of the cocoon, while others do so more openly. Shedding its outer parts, the caterpillar begins digesting its inner parts into a soup of nutrients. Different genes become activated, directing the synthesis of a butterfly from the parts previously assembled into a caterpillar.

Wings develop, often fabulously multi-colored. Stretching out its body and expanding its wings, the newly emergent butterfly waits briefly for its interior fluids to fill its new shape. Within an hour of leaving its cocoon, the former caterpillar has assumed its butterfly form well enough to fly. Its growth stage has finished with the end of its life as a caterpillar. From now on, the butterfly will eat the sugar-water mix called nectar secreted by certain plants, and some butterflies are very finicky in their choice of plant nectars. Sometimes only one plant will be favored. The butterfly's new career becomes reproduction, whereby it will seek a mate and procreate, producing eggs that hatch new caterpillars to eat new leaves and secrete new silken cocoons from which will emerge new butterflies in an endless series of transformations.

During courtship, scent-containing chemicals called pheromones are released like perfumes to attract mates. Dances are performed, with male butterflies hoping that a female will join him in a dance. During the act of copulation, the male not only inserts sperm into the female, but also a nutrient-laden package called a "spermatophore." This contains chemicals gathered by the male from specific flowers or other sources that will greatly increase the viability of the fertilized egg the female will soon lay.

Like caterpillars, toxic or foul-tasting butterflies tend to be brightly colored to warn away predators. Butterflies of other species mimic in color or pattern those toxic butterflies. The colored scales of butterfly wings often have different patterns on top compared to bottom, to create different advertisement or camouflage patterns when seen from below compared to above. A common adornment is the eyespot, an area on a butterfly wing that looks like an eye and may divert a predator to bite the tip of a wing where the eyespot is located rather than the butterfly's head.

Butterflies may live as adults for a couple weeks or a number of months. Monarch butterflies have varying generational times based on the season. The species winters in the wooded highlands of central Mexico. A generation of monarchs, typical lightweight butterflies, not only migrates at times over two thousand miles to reach its destination, but also accurately locates those Mexican highlands despite never having made this flight before. This fantastic journey for such a tiny being, buffeted by winds, lasts for months, and the generation of monarchs that makes this migration lives about nine months. It defers its procreation until shortly before its death and its long journey is finished. Subsequent generations of monarchs come north with the warmer weather in the spring, re-populating North America each year from the winter base in Mexico. The generations that move north and reproduce may live only a month or so. This whole species is under siege by logging in the Mexican highlands that threatens the winter base.

The point is that each butterfly represents a stage in an ongoing series of metamorphoses in which the chemicals of life are transformed from shape to shape. Each phase requires specialized skills, has specialized tasks, and requires specialized knowledge. Each phase is designed to make possible its role fulfillment as it morphs from egg to crawling, dining caterpillar, to pupa in a silken cocoon, to brightly-colored flying butterfly built for mating and migrating.

It all sounds like a fairy tale, in which the kiss of a princess turns a frog into a handsome prince. Yet the presence of butterflies provides proof that their own series of metamorphoses is no fairy tale. All life forms represent metamorphoses, in which earth and air become living bodies; all organisms that eat turn other living things into themselves. Consider the changes in your own body since the day of your birth. Each life form represents a continual metamorphosis of outside elements into the chemicals that make up its body. Your lunch becomes you.

When you see a butterfly, think about the amazing metamorphoses of its life, and how such an organism can be so beautiful to our eyes.

Birds

By the time I was two years old, I had learned that birds fly. This simply is the way the world works, so I never felt surprised when I saw a flying bird. Yet of course, the ability of heavier-than-air objects to fly defied human capability until the last few generations. We now not only fly in planes, but also have learned to ignore the remarkable nature of flying aircraft because it is the routine nature of planes, like birds, to fly. Our minds, with their programming to detect new stimuli in the environment, have adapted to accept and ignore these consciously guided flying objects, both natural and technological. What does it take to attract our attention and sense of wonder?

Think about birds, for example. Obviously they fly, with a specific intent based on their needs and desires. They know everything required to survive and procreate. They don't need pilot training to take their first flight, but leap off into space and spread their wings with an innate trust that the air will support them. With midair directional changes, they avoid hazards and softly land without crashing. They know how to identify, locate, and ingest the foods on which they survive, turning insects, seeds, fruits, or worms into bird flesh and bird flight. They know how to build their own homes, mate, protect their eggs, and create future generations of birds from the atoms of Earth.

Since our minds are on the lookout for the exceptional rather than the commonplace, birds do not disappoint in terms of remarkable exploits. Their migrational skills should draw our amazement. Multiple sources cite a Manx Shearwater that was removed in the 1950s from its burrow on the island of Skokholm in Western Wales and flown to Boston, Massachusetts, where it was released. This pelagic (oceangoing) bird was found back at its original home in Wales 12 and one-half days later. It had flown 3,100 miles across trackless ocean at an average rate of 250 miles per day. The will to return home and the skill and power to accomplish such a journey incite our amazement while defying our understanding.

European storks migrate each autumn to Africa rather than endure European winters. Guided by skills not granted to humans, they typically return each spring to the same nest on the same roof as the previous year. The long-distance champion among migrants is the arctic tern, which hatches in Northern Greenland or Canada in July. With little life experience and no travel experience, the tern sets out within a few weeks on a journey of some 15,000 miles. It will cross the Atlantic, fly along the Western coast of Europe and Africa, and eventually reach the icy realms near the South Pole to spend several months in the Antarctic summer. It will then follow a reverse course to Greenland or Canada as summertime reaches these far northern lands. This lifestyle, so costly in energy expended, gives proof of the arctic terns' survivability with each new generation.

Blackpoll warblers are fast migrants, zipping 2,500 miles from Northern Canada to South America in less than four days. Ruby-throated hummingbirds are tiny migrants, doubling their weight from its baseline of one-tenth of an ounce to a slightly brawnier one-fifth of an ounce in preparation for their flight in late summer from Canada across the Gulf of Mexico to South America.

It is speculated that migrants time their departure dates by what is called photoperiodism, a physiological response to diminishing day length. A particular day-night ratio triggers hormonal changes accompanied by the buildup of fat to serve as fuel for these epic journeys. Their means of staying on track remains poorly understood by our science, though certain factors have been identified, and birds likely shift between different modes of navigation. By day, birds can follow geographical landmarks, by night, stars (though stars provide a moving grid that appears to travel east to west throughout the night due to Earth's rotation). There may be some reliance on Earth's magnetic field. It is presumed that birds also rely on sun position, but this entails a sense of time to compensate for the changing position of the sun relative to the spinning Earth over the course of the day. Though cloudy skies or fog may obscure navigational landmarks, somehow birds still manage to reach targets hundreds or thousands of miles away, even small islands in the middle of oceans. The direction of prevailing winds may be navigationally helpful, and may also be utilized as a source of power to carry the birds onward. David Attenborough, British naturalist and filmmaker, states in admiration, "So it seems that many migrating birds must carry in their brains a clock, a compass, and the memory of a map." [103] This applies even if the bird has never taken the journey before.

There are many different migration strategies. Some species tend to fly low at perhaps 500-1,150 feet, and even lower during storms. This affords the opportunity to descend to Earth for rest and feeding. Some travel by day, some by night, some continuously for thousands of miles. Large birds like ducks and geese often fly higher (ducks and geese frequently migrate around the clock, at heights that may exceed one mile), and night-flyers tend to fly higher than daytime migrants. Night flight and greater height during travel may increase exposure to the elements, but reduce exposure to predators. Some birds are solitary migrants; some travel in flocks, seeking relative safety in numbers.

Even within a species, variations in strategy may occur. There are birds that might only migrate short distances, perhaps one hundred or a few hundred miles, while others, especially in the era of bird feeders, might not choose to migrate at all. Gardening columnist and ornithologist Pierre Gingras cites Frank B. Gill's estimate that about 10 billion birds migrate each year, greater than the entire human population of the planet. [104] Approximately half of the long-distance migrants travel between Europe or Asia at the northern terminus to Africa in the south, while most of the rest travel the Americas, from Canada or the United States to Mexico and Central or South America.

The toll of these arduous journeys on such small animals can be enormous. Gingras states that of the 100 million ducks and geese that migrate south each winter, fewer than half return, with a particularly high toll on first-time migrants. [105] Predators, storms, accidents, and exhaustion thin the ranks. Yet migration from climates with bitter winters is overall a more successful survival strategy for many species than taking the risk of overwintering at home. Not only can the cold itself kill, but traditional food sources such as seeds and insects become rare. Bird feeders now encourage more birds to take the gamble of lasting out the winter at home, which leaves them, should they survive, with first pick of nesting and feeding sites well in advance of the returning migrants.

One question to consider with the next bird you see would be where he or she has traveled. Did they visit Africa or South America, travel a couple hundred miles south for the winter, or just hang around the neighborhood? Obviously their strategy worked, because here they are.

While we are acknowledging the exceptional rather than the routine gifts possessed by birds, we might consider May 27, 1784. That was the date Mozart purchased a starling in a pet shop because it sang, presumably in imitation, part of Mozart's Piano Concerto Number 17 in G major. It is speculated that Mozart at some time might have whistled or hummed the melody in the bird's presence, and the bird memorized it and sang it back to him.

If you sit on your porch and close your eyes, you will become aware of the prevalence of bird songs all around you. Typical calls involve five or fewer notes, with a duration of perhaps four seconds (rarely greater than 10 seconds), and the singer is usually a male. He is presumably announcing his species and location to rival males in defense of his territory, and inviting females to come visit. Older birds tend to develop more elaborate melodies, but the singer tends to focus less on variety (after all, he doesn't want to be misidentified) than on repetition. Over and over he announces a similar message and a similar song, though some species such as mockingbirds have a broader repertoire. A song sparrow was documented repeating his song over 2,300 times in one day by a presumably bored researcher, and the one-day record reported by Gingras was a Red-eyed Vireo whose 22,197 repetitions will be hard to beat. [106]

Singing begins before dawn, declines over the course of the morning, then resumes during the latter part of the afternoon and evening. Birds with the showiest feathers tend to use those feathers as a means of communicating their presence, especially in open areas. In the woods where it is more difficult for a bird to be seen (and the bird likely prefers not to be overly visible), it is more likely to rely on songs for communication. The greatest bird vocalists tend to be visually inconspicuous with bland coloration.

Hone in closer regarding some of the other remarkable features and variations birds possess. Flying birds, like supermodels, must keep their weight down. They use several mechanisms to accomplish this; much of the interior of their body is composed of lungs and air sacs. Their bones are thin and hollow, and they do not have teeth or jawbones at all. With no teeth for chewing, birds use an internal gizzard to grind up their food so they can digest it. The gizzard is located near the center of the bird, so its balance while flying will not be affected by a recent meal.

Bird feathers, bills, and claws are made from strong but lightweight keratin, the substance that makes our fingernails and toenails. The feathers actually weigh two to three times more than the bones in an average bird. A typical small backyard bird might have 2,000-4,000 feathers. Each feather has a central shaft from which approximately one hundred filaments emerge on each side; "… each filament is similarly fringed with about a hundred smaller filaments or barbules." [107] In feathers, the barbules overlap with the barbules on adjacent filaments and hook into them to create a single continuous unit. "There are several hundred such hooks on a single barbule, a million or so in a single feather; and a bird the size of a swan has about twenty-five thousand feathers." [108]

These feathers provide warmth (think of a down comforter filled with such feathers) and are waterproof. Most birds even come equipped with an oil gland near their tail. With their beak, they extract this oil and spread it on their feathers to maintain their insulating and waterproofing qualities. The feathers also provide identification through which birds recognize each other. Typically birds will molt or shed and replace their feathers at least once a year in a gradual process. This allows them to match their feathers to the seasons, often displaying bright colors in the springtime when mating and romance are in the air, while blending in with less conspicuous colors during the rest of the year to minimize the attentions of potential predators. Before migrations, new strong feathers replace the old and aged ones. In winter, birds tend to grow a denser plumage; on cold nights, they tuck their heads under their wings and their feet under their feathers, and sometimes cluster together for mutual warmth.

Their bills or beaks are also made of keratin; this substance constantly wears down but continually regenerates, just as our fingernails continue to grow. Bills have a wide variety of shapes remarkably well-adapted to their function. A hummingbird has a long thin bill to extract nectar from flowers. A woodpecker uses his powerful beak like a hammer or a drill. A chickadee uses a small pointed beak to crack small seeds; a macaw employs a mighty beak to split open Brazil nuts. Flamingos have a long curved bill to strain water for crustaceans.

Claws also are adapted to function, from the fierce grasping talons of birds of prey to claws better suited to clutching branches for most of the birds that come to the feeder. Flight is a high-energy activity, requiring warm-blooded birds to eat high calorie foods, while avoiding obesity that would prevent them from flying. Pay attention to the huge variations in bird shapes, sizes, and body features - at this moment they are all looking for food in and around your yard, so your neighborhood must offer a wide variety of potential food sources and effective bird habitats.

Wings must also fit the bird's lifestyle and meet its need for efficiency, speed, and maneuverability. Small backyard birds and forest birds prize maneuverability above speed, and require short wings to make tight turns between branches without getting tangled. Hawks and vultures rely on broad rectangular wings to slowly glide over uprising air. Falcon wings are positioned to sweep backward, allowing the bird to rapidly accelerate forward. Hummingbird wings traverse figure-of-eight patterns at an average rate of perhaps 50 beats per second, driving the air downward on both the forward and backward stroke, enabling the bird to hover at the same spot in midair while sipping nectar from flowers. Gliding birds such as the albatross have long thin wings, allowing them to fly for several hours without ever beating their wings. Birds flying over open sea are more likely to have long wings that provide more distance with each beat, since they are generally flying through unobstructed sky. Swifts, aptly named, fly up to 170 kilometers per hour, covering some 600 miles per day eating insects, staying in continuous flight at least nine months per year, and even copulating in mid-air. For this demanding lifestyle, its wings are so long that it cannot beat them properly while on the ground and must instead launch itself from a cliff or its nest to get enough room to fully flap its wings.

Birds, like squirrels, bury seeds, and we owe many of our trees to the inability of these parties to remember all the burial sites. This is not surprising since quite a few seeds are buried. Someone had the patience to count 50,000 seeds placed underground by a tufted titmouse during one autumn, and 150,000 beechnuts buried by blue jays over 23 days. These seeds will help many a bird and squirrel survive the winter and result in many a tree being inadvertently born to serve as a home for future birds and squirrels as part of the mutual relationship between trees and the animals that inhabit them.

No good saga is complete without a romantic angle, and birds are no exception. Gingras tells us: "The 'love life' of birds is rather turbulent. It is punctuated by winged pursuit, intimidation, interminable song, dance, aerial acrobatics, even intimate dinners."[109] Males choose and defend a territory, then face the age-old problem of trying to attract a female. They sing, strut their plumage, perhaps engage in courtship dances that can be dazzling, and might even offer their potential mate a tasty insect or caterpillar. If all this attracts a willing female, the male still faces the anatomic problem of lacking external genitalia (which if present could cause some uncomfortable landings in a flying species). Hence, though courtship may be prolonged over days or even weeks, intercourse is awkward and brief. The male latches onto the back of his mate, the two align their genital openings, and both work together to spill the sperm from the male into the female. Most birds are monogamous at least through the breeding season, though some - geese, cranes, penguins, ravens, crows, and flamingos, for example - form long-term and perhaps life-long bonds.

Staying together is useful, because the eggs require constant attention. Since they are a high-energy food source and defenseless, unguarded eggs can provide a quick meal for a predator. Hence one bird, more often the female, must guard the eggs. The other, more likely the male, must make multiple forays from the nest to obtain and bring back food. Such roles can be switched. The nest itself is a protective structure that birds intuitively know how to construct. A bird typically builds one nest per year in the spring, but may build more if the pair have more than one brood. Nest building usually lasts between a few days and a few weeks, depending on the species. There is often some attempt to conceal or at least camouflage the nest during this dangerous time when a bird cannot simply fly away from a predator without abandoning its offspring.

Because sperm remain viable within the female for a few weeks, she can produce multiple fertilized eggs from a single intercourse. Birds can lay no more than one egg every one to two days, and they incubate over two to six weeks, depending on the species and size of the bird. When the eggs have been laid, they are incubated beneath either parent and hatch typically within hours of each other. All those birds in your yard were once in eggs, hatched successfully, and are either paired with a mate or seeking one. All know how to build a nest, and have a strategy to survive through the winter.

The eggs that are produced are dotted with pores, 7,000 in a typical hen's egg, through which the atmospheric gases and water vapor of the outside world enter. The eggshell thins out over time as its calcium is absorbed into the bones of the embryo. On the day of its birth, the embryo uses an "egg-tooth" on its upper mandible to crack open the shell and exit into the outside world. After employing its instinctive knowledge to chew its way out of the shell, the newborn bird finds itself in a nest with siblings, one or two parents, and a remarkable instinctive knowledge of how to act like a bird.

Birds at birth are classified as precocial or altricial. Precocial birds are not fed by their parents, but have the skills to survive immediately on their own, though parents may help a little at the start. Precocial ducks jump to the ground from nests as high as 55 feet and usually land comfortably. Seabirds take the leap of faith from nests on high promontories to the sea perhaps 100 yards below. On the other hand, altricial birds like robins, wrens, and chickadees, are typically born scrawny with closed eyes, and require initial parental protection and feeding before launching themselves into the air. This requires harder work for the parents, who have more mouths to feed and defend. Yet the birds instinctively know what to do; the parents offer food and protection, while the offspring know when and how to fly from the nest into their own independent life. [110] [111]

When I was in school, the sort of instinctive knowledge possessed by the animal kingdom was viewed as a lesser way of knowing than the logical understanding our cerebral cortex affords. Yet it is difficult not to be amazed by birds. Throughout the world, they discover a way to turn almost any environment into their restaurant and a place to live. They choose solitary or group or mated lifestyles, stay home or travel thousands of miles as small wind-blown creatures who likely do not even understand the restlessness that sends them southward at a particular season through skies that have no paths. How do they know when or with whom to mate, why a particular song or feather pattern is so exciting, and how, when, and where to build a nest? What is passing through their minds when they first step to the edge of the nest, spread their untested wings, and sail into space?

Sometimes I fantasize how I might feel to have the instinctive certainties of a migrating bird traveling over unknown terrain but confidently knowing the way. What must it be like to take the leap into space for the first time with the confidence that your wings will take you wherever you choose, trusting that you already know where to go?

Why are we denied such certainties? We as humans live in a hazy world, heavily immersed in its artificialities, not necessarily aware of the limits of our logic.

Yet I sit on the back porch or walk around the block, treating every bird I see as a door that opens into a realm of mystery. The processes of Earth mold - and are molded into - the body of a bird. In the form of a bird, the atoms of Earth take flight.

How does it know what it knows, and do what it does? In plain sight, a bird invites you to meditate on its existence, and yours.

Clouds

Look up. Clouds are floating by overhead. They provide a rapid demonstration that processes clothe themselves in changing forms. The cloud that looked like a cat three minutes ago has morphed into a dragon and floated a little farther downwind on its path toward growth or dissolution. Its precious cargo is water, now in droplets that have condensed on nuclei of dust from the land or salt from the sea. While visibly clear air also carries water, the increased water density within a cloud makes the otherwise invisible apparent to our eyes.

Drawn upward from Earth by the evaporative heat of the Sun, the water is taking a ride across the atmosphere before eventually precipitating back to Earth. The rain will be cheered by farmers and cursed by prospective picnickers and golfers. The disdain that many people feel toward rain seems strange considering that living organisms such as ourselves are made of water. In cursing rain, we curse our primary ingredient. What is life on Earth if not a complex dance of water from one form to another? The solid earth and liquid rain transmute each other, and we are one of the transmutations.

William Least Heat-Moon in *PrairyErth* relates his own vision as he gazes upon Kansas sedimentary rock that formed from the remains of once-living organisms that inhabited the area when it was covered by sea long ago, where today there flows only a small creek: "... the wind carries in the rain, the water flushes along organic acids that eat the permeable stone back into liquid and send it again toward the far father sea; the solids come in and head out, just pausing; all around me are absorptions and percolations, everything soluble, the grasses sucking the mutable rock and transpiring, everything between forms of liquidity, and all things forms of liquidity...." [112] The clouds above us and our own bodies are temporary forms that water takes.

Loren Eiseley, anthropologist and philosopher, expressed his own vision in *The Immense Journey*: "I was water and the unspeakable alchemies that gestate and take shape in water ... Turtle and fish and the pinpoint chirpings of individual frogs are all water projections, concentrations - as man himself is a concentration - of that indescribable and liquid brew which is compounded in varying proportions of salt and sun and time." [113]

From the clouds, rain falls onto Earth, and part of it is incorporated into the millions of species of living organisms. Much of the rest cuts and carves and dissolves the rock and soil of Earth, before being drawn down creeks to rivers and onward to the sea. From all waterways, all oceans, and from the bodies of organisms such as the plants and animals on the surface of our planet - including ourselves - the Sun's heat draws water back into the atmosphere, back into new clouds to float where they will and rain down their cargo.

Think about the long history of individual water molecules in the cloud currently above you. Think of the living organisms they have been part of, the rivers they have traveled, the oceans they have visited, over and over again. Is it raining? The water that so recently was part of that cloud is soaking the soil and entering the roots of grass, trees, and flowers. Any animals that eat the plants will become the new if temporary home to those water molecules. Who knows what forms the water will enter before being drawn once more by the Sun's heat into the atmosphere to again become part of a cloud?

The water molecules within our body, in our cells and our bloodstream, have likewise made many journeys from Earth to sky, from land to air to cloud to river to ocean, being part of many bodies over the long course of time. Now part of that water is within us, and part is in the cloud, but this arrangement is temporary. Clouds are not merely our brothers - they contain past and future components of ourselves.

Watch a cloud for a few minutes. Watch it change shape against the backdrop of the ancient sky.

Waves

Ocean waves are the product of wind blowing across water, of one natural process shaping another. Pull up a chair, sit on the beach, watch the dance. Before lapping against your feet, the wave may have traversed an ocean across 1,000 miles or more. Yet no specific "piece" of water made that journey; rather individual water molecules travel in a small, roughly circular path while transmitting the wave disturbance to the next "piece" of water, and the wave disturbance gets transmitted from piece to piece until it reaches shore. The structural composition of the wave changes with every moment, involving a given area of water only temporarily before moving on to the next area.

How "real" is the wave? We can take a picture of the wave with our camera and label it "wave" in our scrapbook, but two pictures of the wave taken five seconds apart will depict a completely different set of water molecules constituting the wave in the second picture compared to the first one. The wave is real as a process but not as a distinct structure.

Many types of waves pass through the universe. There are waves flowing through apparently solid land, folding Earth into mountain ranges, some of whose peaks are called the Himalayas. There are waves passing through the air, generating storms and wind. There are sound waves, light waves; there are waves flowing through the vast hydrogen clouds of space, creating galaxies. There are unseen waves flowing through atoms, somehow giving shape to the visible universe.

Forms at all scales of time and distance arise as the transient physical manifestation of processes. No part of nature exists as a thing-in-and-of-itself. It is differential heating of Earth by the sun that generates the wind that drives the waves that carve the cliffs that are dissolved by rivers that flow to the sea.

From our beach chair, we cannot watch galaxies form or mountains rise as energy flows through the universe and gives it shape. Their scale is too vast and slow for human perception. We can, however, watch waves after their journey through the ocean reach the shore and dissipate, surrendering their water molecules to be drawn into future waves, or evaporated into clouds to turn into distant raindrops.

Pull up a chair, bask in the sun, and watch the waves.

There really is only one planetary ocean, though it is known by different names - such as Atlantic or Pacific - in different geographic regions. This is like giving separate names to different parts of the same body. Individual water molecules traverse from "ocean" to "ocean," from the surface to the depths, from the tropics to the poles, and back again, before giving a lift to your surfboard. In its travels, the ocean water transmits heat from the tropics to the poles, and in doing so, reduces temperature extremes over the planet. It also ties up chemicals like carbon and calcium in the shells and bodies of sea creatures, affecting the chemistry and climate of the continents. With its currents, the ocean distributes nutrients that determine the distribution of living organisms. Each water molecule is in the midst of an epic journey as it dances around your feet in the waves.

The power behind the waves typically comes from the Sun, which heats some parts of the world more than others, causing temperature and pressure differences within the air, driving the air to move, creating wind. The lowest levels of moving air skim the top of the ocean, humping the surface into waves. Differential solar heating also sets up currents and eddies within the sea, propelling water molecules from the surface to the depths and around the globe. Hence the story of the wind and waves is partly the story of the Sun.

Another co-director of the scene is the Moon, whose gravity steers the tides. There are two high tides and two low tides each day, courtesy of the Moon. The higher of the two high tides occurs as the Moon, in passing over your beach in its orbit around the Earth, gravitationally draws the waters of the single Earth ocean moonward, pulling water up to its highest mark on the beach in doing so. This high tide circles the planet each day, following the Moon. The lower of the two daily high tides occurs on the side of the Earth that is opposite from the Moon, as a sort of "slingshot effect" hurls water to the far side of the Earth as well.

If your beach is a typical one, you have tossed your blanket on sand. Waves that have pounded the shoreline through the eons have chewed up the original shoreline rock into the tiny grains from which we make sand castles today, and on which your blanket rests. The exact chemical structure of the sand varies based on which type of shore rock was being slammed by the waves, but silicon is a common chemical of Earth's crust and therefore a common component of sand grains on the beach. The tough remnant after the rest of the rock has been pulverized is this silica, whose grains provide a soft cushion under the beach towel.

Hence the Sun and Moon, acting on the Earth, create wind-driven ocean waves that wash up onto sandy beaches while distributing heat, nutrients, and energy around the planet. Huge forces have been at work in crafting such a nice, relaxing day at the beach, just the right place to toss a towel and take a swim.

Grass

How does a blade of grass grow? Start with seeds or tufts from the previous generation and insert into the ground. The recipe requires the planet Earth, into which the grass sends its roots to withdraw the elements that will compose it. Also required is water to dissolve and transport those elements into the blade we are contemplating. We see the slender green shoot above ground, our visual conceptualization of "grass;" below the surface out of sight lie the roots. In 1937, a scientist dug up a two-year-old tuft of grass and dissected, in four cubic meters of loam, a root system that extended 315 miles. [114]

The Earth has undergone some preparation, pre-packaging the elements that can come to life after condensing out of a gas cloud in space a congenial distance from the nearest star. The water itself has been many places and recycled many times. Most recently it evaporated hundreds or thousands of miles away, perhaps from an ocean, and was carried on the wind to your neighborhood, where it fell as rain from clouds to Earth under the influence of gravity. Because gravity will prove useful in attracting the rain and allowing the seeds and grass to stick to the planet, having access to a universe with the appropriate laws of nature and physics will be necessary for grass to exist. Those laws will prove handy again in generating breezes that spread grass seed around the planet.

Some cooking will be required, so a Sun that fuses hydrogen to helium will suffice. Our universe is very adept at generating suns, so the universe you live in should be adequate for growing a blade of grass. Temperature control is important; the grass can suffer damage through being scorched or frozen, so avoiding huge extremes of temperature is advisable.

Add in some carbon dioxide gas for the grass to inhale from the air. With proper light and heat, the grass has an internal mechanism for converting the water and carbon dioxide to carbohydrates that provide the energy for its life, while yielding oxygen back into the atmosphere. The presence of animals on the planet should prove helpful as they exhale back into the air the very carbon dioxide the blade of grass requires.

Scour the planet to find the micronutrients the grass will need, or simply buy them as fertilizer from someone else who has scoured the planet, and water those ingredients into the ground from time to time. The sun will draw the water and dissolved nutrients from the roots into the blade via a natural internal elevator system that you will not need to install. Water periodically. With the proper alignment of the forces of the universe, you should have an excellent blade of grass to admire and contemplate.

Simply pick the right universe, the right nearby star at an appropriate distance, the right planet, the right laws of nature and physics, bury some grass seed into the dirt, and follow the recipe. Most of the challenging work has already been done. If you allow yourself to be the agent through whom a new blade of grass grows, meditate upon the enormity of your accomplishment and the boundless generosity of the universe. You can perform this meditation while mowing the lawn, because the grass will have an internal drive to continue growing all summer.

Wonderland

Our brains are on the lookout for novelty and are programmed to filter out the ordinary. It requires intentional mindfulness to find magic in the commonplace, since the commonplace is, after all, common. A rabbit's hole is just a rabbit's hole until Alice falls through it into Wonderland.

To pick a suitable subject for your meditation, look anywhere. If what you see is technological, consider the creative possibilities of our 3-pound brain. If it is a natural feature of Earth, think about its cosmic history and the forces that have shaped it. If it is living, recognize that Earth has generated organisms that know how to survive and reproduce. Open your window shades and observe some of the millions of species formed from the atoms of our fertile planet. Give your awareness free rein.

Almost anything, when thoughtfully considered by your miraculous mind, just might be your entry into Wonderland.

YOU

Dr. Sanderson to Elwood P. Dowd: "We all have to face reality, Dowd – sooner or later."

Elwood P. Dowd to Dr. Sanderson: "Doctor, I wrestled with reality for forty years, and I am happy to state that I finally won out over it."

Mary Chase
Harvey

seeker of truth

follow no path
all paths lead where

truth is here

e. e. cummings
73 poems

Let me know myself, Lord, and I shall know Thee.

St. Augustine

Arbitrary Assumptions

In the old Superman comic books and television shows of my childhood, Clark Kent would enter a phone booth in the persona of a mild-mannered newspaper reporter and emerge transformed into mighty Superman, "able to leap tall buildings in a single bound." Of course, the dual character knew his real identity was always Superman, and that the Clark Kent persona was merely a disguise to keep his superpowers hidden. Most of us have the reverse problem - we think we are only Clark Kent and are unaware that our real capabilities are in a true sense superpowers.

In the large city in which I live, I have not met anyone who aspires to be a beggar or live in a cave, although such choices would not be unusual in some of the world's cultures. Behavior within a culture is driven by shared assumptions and shared values, which typically have historical origins and may or may not be universally true. Our world is infinitely complex; ultimately, we cannot understand it. Rather than wander around lost, we create models of reality, man-made constructs. Each culture creates a different model, a different map by which to navigate in that culture. As long as a person stays within a homogeneous culture, surrounded by people who accept and perpetuate the same model, it seems as if the model is independently true.

One of the main features of Western society's model is the assumption that a key objective of a typical day should be to advance socio-economically. This idea rests on the presumption that "more is better," and leads to the conclusion that it is in our best interest to sacrifice the present for the future. However, to seek a higher rung on the ladder of success is to devalue our current rung and overvalue what we lack.

In the mirror right now, what you see is yourself, the basic unit, your gift from the universe. Does the image that you perceive appear small and bounded, or miraculous? If you only see your limits in that mirror image, you are driven toward obtaining additional accessories, often at a steep price. American transcendentalist Henry David Thoreau in *Walden* reminds us that in the end what we sacrifice in every purchase is the chunk of our lives that we give up in trade. [115] The ability to perceive a talented and amazing individual in the mirror changes our strategy from battling to obtain what we don't have to appreciating what we already are.

Certainly some sacrifices and battles are worthwhile, but we must choose them wisely. If I view my life as a struggle between me, weighing 175 pounds or about 80 kilograms versus the rest of the world, with a mass of 6,000,000,000,000,000,000,000,000 kilograms and 7 billion other people, I am outweighed and outmanned. I can make my life less stressful and more beautiful by re-choosing sides. If I recognize that I, like you, am a very remarkable being, I can reasonably view the world as being on my team as it sustains my existence. Eastern philosophy conveys this concept as "Te," translated as "Virtuality," representing the capabilities we have been granted by virtue of being human. We are about to explore some of our "superpowers."

By recognizing our miraculous nature, we can let go of many of the battles that seem to be an unavoidable feature of life. Indian mystic (and Rolls-Royce fancier) Osho writes, "If you see that the stones that you have carried all this time are not real diamonds, what are you going to do with them? It will not need great courage to drop them, to throw them away ... You were not clinging to those stones, but to the idea that they were diamonds. You were clinging to your fallacy, your illusion." [116]

We are all experts at detecting the imperfections in our lives, and have waged war on them, judging our days by the unachievable standard of perfection. This, too, is a feature of Western culture and not universal. Obviously we should strive to do our best but should not be shocked by the imperfections that pervade all human enterprise. Eastern philosophy has different expectations with its concept of yin and yang. Yang represents the positive pole of creation, yin the negative. As a leading figure in introducing Zen and Taoism to Western audiences, Alan Watts in multiple writings stresses that positives and negatives should not be thought of as conflicting, but rather as the two poles of real world situations. North has no meaning without south, and happiness has no meaning without unhappiness. [117] [118] To demand only positives is to guarantee disappointment. The expectation that a car or an air conditioner or a human life will always be perfect denies the true nature of each. Perfection is an abstract concept. It is not the stuff from which human lives are formed.

The strategy of continually sacrificing the present for the future ultimately breaks down, because in a sense, the future never comes. Each day as it arrives becomes "today," which a future-focused lifestyle dictates should be sacrificed on behalf of days that have not yet come.

Spiritual teacher Eckhart Tolle in *The Power of Now* states, "Nothing ever happened in the past; it happened in the Now. Nothing will ever happen in the future; it will happen in the Now." [119] To Tolle, the present moment takes on deep spiritual significance: "The eternal present is the space within which your whole life unfolds ... Now is the only point that can take you beyond the limited confines of the mind. It is your only point of access into the timeless and formless realm of Being." [120]

We spend so much of our life and energy trying to battle our way from here and now to there and later, when the most important journey each of us will ever take is the journey of perception from the mundane "here" to the miraculous "here."

As New England poet Mary Oliver advises in "Wild Geese":

> You do not have to walk on your knees
> For a hundred miles through the desert repenting.
> You only have to let the soft animal of your body
> Love what it loves. [121]

You must also *be aware* that you love what you love. It is this awareness that takes us on the transformative journey to the "here" of enchantment. Recognize your amazing nature, celebrate this moment, and love what you love.

Age

Are you feeling mature today? You should. In a sense, your age is approximately 13.7 billion years. Although your birth was considerably more recent, you are composed of 13.7-billion-year-old parts. Don't feel alone on this, since everything in the universe is as old as you.

Our universe is thought to have originated in the explosive creation of pure energy in an event called the Big Bang, judged by current scientific theory to have occurred that long ago. It is unknown what, if anything, existed before that. The energy involved in the Big Bang has been morphing into new combinations ever since, and everything that has ever existed, including the mightiest galaxies and all living things on Earth, represent transmutations of that original energy. As Brian Cox and Andrew Cohen put it in *Wonders of the Universe*, "Every piece of every one and every thing you love, of every thing you hate, of every thing you hold precious, was assembled in the first few minutes of the Universe, and transformed in the hearts of stars or created in their fiery deaths." [122]

Every present-day mountain range and feather is considered a transformation of that ancient energy. We are all refurbished - 13.7 billion-year-old ingredients that were previously in stars and interstellar space drifted for those billions of years before being re-packaged to form our bodies. Again I quote Cox and Cohen, "When we look out into space we are looking at our place of birth. We truly are children of the stars, and written into every atom and molecule of our bodies is the history of the universe, from the Big Bang to the present day." [123] Every atom now in our body took that vast interstellar journey. When our parents in an act of passion contributed one cell each - a sperm and an egg - that cell carried the DNA blueprint leading to our creation from the elements of the cosmos on the planet Earth in the Milky Way Galaxy.

The entire landscape we walk through, and the energy that powers us, are equally ancient. Nothing is tossed out by Nature; no part is locked eternally in any particular form. All forms are ultimately transient, so we should not feel unique in our own transience either. Do you feel any different knowing that in a sense your age is measured in billions of years rather than decades? As you look around you, consider that this world generates from such ancient stuff this wild variety of new forms, and one of them is you.

Stardust

Our body is a collection of elements that somehow have come to life. Atoms such as the iron and nitrogen in our bodies were part of the Earth and its atmosphere before they became part of us. Before that, they were part of the stars, and part of the gas clouds of interstellar space. Plants, growing out of Earth, incorporate planetary chemicals that then enter the bodies of animals that eat the plants. We are what we eat and what we breathe, taking in chemicals to synthesize our body. Each atom has a remarkable story to tell.

Joel R. Primack and Nancy Ellen Abrams in *The View from the Center of the Universe* summarize the history of some of the elements of the cosmic cookbook. They relate that, "... the iron atoms in our blood carrying oxygen at this moment to our cells came largely from exploding white dwarf stars, while the oxygen itself came mainly from exploding supernovas that ended the lives of massive stars, and most of the carbon in the carbon dioxide we exhale on every breath came from the planetary nebulas, the death clouds of middle-sized stars a little bigger than the sun." [124]

Primack and Abrams continue, "It is huge stars more than about eight times the mass of the sun that produce most of the oxygen and neon and all the really heavy elements ... In the terminal processes of such stars (after becoming red giants), their centers develop an onion-like structure, with hydrogen fusing in an outer layer, helium in a deeper layer, then carbon, neon, oxygen, with silicon and sulfur fusing in the core. Eventually the core becomes mostly iron, the most tightly bound nucleus, and then further fusion is impossible." [125]

Other atoms that are now within us had different primary sources in the astronomical foundry. "Medium-sized stars more massive than our sun produced the medium-weight atoms like carbon and nitrogen that make up more than 20% of the weight of your body." [126] Terminal explosions of ancient stars broadcast these elements into the blackness of interstellar space, where they drifted for untold eons. Under the influence of gravity, in our small neighborhood in a giant universe, atoms from such disparate sources swirled and gathered, became our solar system, became Earth, became us.

Primack and Abrams summarize: "... later generations of stars like our sun contain mixtures of elements built up from many supernovas and planetary nebulas, and our planet is made of the same varieties of atoms. Stardust is thus part of our genealogy. Our bodies literally hold the entire history of the universe, witnessed and enacted by our atoms." [127] Incredibly, the birthplace of every atom in our body is extraterrestrial.

A friend of William Bryant Logan, recognizing the origin of the atoms that compose us, came to the realization that, "We are all stardust." Logan's analysis goes a step further, "In fact, *everything* is stardust." [128]

Noodles

No one really understands the origin of the universe, the original mystery. Though Western civilization has generally envisioned this as the sudden creation of a universe from a pre-existing void, it is also possible that we inhabit a universe that is a small part of a much larger "multiverse," whose ultimate nature is unknown. If one universe can exist or be created, why not others?

Primack and Abrams explore the implications of a multiverse, in which our own universe would be one among many. "In fact," they state, "Instead of starting our origin stories 'In the beginning ...' we may need to humble the phrase to 'In a beginning ...' which is an equally accurate translation of the Hebrew word 'bereshit' at the beginning of the Bible. Or we can simply say, 'In our beginning.'" [129]

The currently prevailing Big Bang Theory posits that our universe burst into existence from a single point. In traditional cosmology and many current theologies, that point was in a void. In multiverse theory, the point was within a pre-existing "something" from which universes emerge.

Let us veer for a moment from speculative concepts of the unknowable to a literary work of fantasy. In the short story "All at One Point" from his book *Cosmicomics*, Italo Calvino depicts fictional characters who were living in a theoretical pre-Big Bang universe in which everything that existed was situated at a single point. Obviously, in the true history of the universe, no living organisms could exist under such conditions. In this science fiction tale, the premise is that all the characters were superimposed on each other at that one point, beyond which there was only nothingness. Amongst them was a good-hearted woman who wished she could cook noodles for the others, if she only had the space to do so. The narrator begins contemplating how much space would be required to prepare those noodles: "... we thought of the space that the flour would occupy, and the wheat for the flour, and the fields to raise the wheat, and the mountains from which the water would flow to irrigate the fields, and the grazing lands for the herds of calves that would give their meat for the sauce; of the space it would take for the Sun to arrive with its rays, to ripen the wheat; of the space for the Sun to condense from the clouds of stellar gases and burn; of the quantities of stars and galaxies and galactic masses in flight through space which would be needed to hold suspended every galaxy, every nebula, every sun, every planet ..." [130]

In short, the space needed to make noodles is ultimately an entire universe, or possibly an entire multiverse, with gas clouds spawning galaxies, which in turn spawn stars and planets that give rise to noodles. Every meal likewise requires a universe and countless eons for its preparation. In fact, the entire history of the universe has been spent giving rise to your next meal - and you. The saga continues as those noodles, in preparation since the dawn of time, become incorporated into the living body of those who eat them for tonight's dinner.

How much space did it take to make you? An entire universe.

How much time was required for your creation? The entire history of the universe.

When you dine on those noodles, think of the galaxies that were required in the preparation of the noodles - and of you.

Remodeling Day

Many a building or office is intermittently closed for remodeling. The same thing happens to roads, which must be closed to be repaved. With our body, no closures are allowed, yet it is constantly changing. We are hardly a finished product when we are born, weighing about 7 pounds. Instead, throughout our life we are always in the process of becoming something that we have never been before.

Although we celebrate our birthday each year by blowing out candles and eating a piece of cake, we certainly existed with the same DNA doing its creative tricks the day before our emergence from our mother, and the day before that. New combinations of genes express themselves, and new life experiences have shaped us every moment since.

With each meal, we ingest elements to maintain and upgrade our infrastructure. Each meal also supplies us with new chemical compounds, like refilling a car's fuel tank with energy-rich gasoline. We are continuously remade with new materials and recharged with new energy.

Similarly, our brain allows memories from the past to dissipate if we do not continually refresh them. Brain memory circuitry that was once used to memorize the names of sixth-grade classmates or mathematical formulas is freed up over time, and then re-used to encode new memories and learn new skills. To an important extent, we determine the mental abilities we will have in the future by the brain hook-ups that we develop and maintain along the way.

For our journey through life, we do not bring with us a lot of luggage to meet our future needs. Rather we have DNA in each cell that gives our bodies the natural wisdom to continually remodel in response to life's challenges. Through our experiences, we retool our brain and body as we develop new skills to face the present and future.

Each day we are "Open For Remodeling."

Buried Treasure

There is a legend about a peasant who dreams of becoming rich. In his dream, the fortune that awaits him is at the King's palace in the distant capital city. Deciding that being a peasant is not a great career choice, he elects to follow his dream. After an arduous journey, he arrives at the King's palace, but is denied admittance by one of the guards. The peasant pleads with the guard that he must be allowed into the palace because his dream was so vivid and his need for buried treasure so acute.

The guard scoffs, saying he never puts any faith in dreams. In fact, he had recently dreamed of buried treasure himself, but doesn't believe in such silliness. Yet as the guard describes where the treasure was buried in his (the guard's) dream, the peasant recognizes the description perfectly fits his own yard back home. Returning home, the peasant starts digging in his own yard at the spot where the treasure was located in the guard's dream. There indeed he finds buried treasure, and presumably lives happily ever after, as fairy-tale characters so often do.

One can draw a variety of morals from this fable. Perhaps, following dreams is not so outlandish as it might seem. Further, the solution to one person's quest can be discovered in another person's experience. However, the central point seems to revolve around the fact that the treasure was ultimately found right at home and had been present but hidden there all along. In a sense, the treasure had always been there for the peasant; it was not treasure that he lacked, but the knowledge of that treasure.

If we are aware that we have treasure right at home, we don't need to go on long, difficult journeys pleading with the apparent guardians of treasure, feeling like outsiders hoping to be allowed in. If we, like the peasant, recognize the miraculous treasure we already have, then we need not travel or beg to lead rich lives. The key to our treasure may not be found entirely in our own dreams; it may be found partly through the words and dreams of others.

Abundance

We often tend to think of our life in terms of what it is denying us. Artist and writer Julia Cameron in *The Artist's Way* suggests we focus instead on life's luxuries. By this she does not mean an expensive automobile or home. The world is immensely generous if we think about luxuries in the right way. She tells of someone who has a passion for music. [131] There is almost no limit to how much music a person can listen to if he chooses.

We are granted on average many thousands of days in a lifetime, each a creative opportunity. Think of the number of meals we will eat over that time, each a true sacrament in a real sense. Recognize that the slice of bread you are eating now will become the blood and body of you, and that you can perform this sacrament in a way you choose day after day.

The number of people we can incorporate in our life is limitless. Ultimately the biggest determinant of a person's happiness is the set of meaningful interpersonal interactions he or she maintains. There is no restriction on the number or depth of our relationships; we each in the next few minutes could talk to a neighbor or co-worker to develop a friendship. Love is also limitless - you don't have a fixed amount that requires careful allotment.

What are your passions? Can you identify passions that are readily available to you, evidence of the world's generosity? Cameron speaks of how artists can be more creative and productive when they feel empowered by this sense of abundance. We are all artists in this way, and each day is a creative act. Today is one of those thousands and thousands of days that serve as a canvas on which we create our life, and the next meal or conversation is another creative process for the artist within us. If we trivialize the meal or the conversation, we deny ourselves a life of abundance.

Look around, Annie Dillard advises us. "If the landscape reveals one certainty, it is that the extravagant gesture is the very stuff of creation. After the one extravagant gesture of creation in the first place, the universe has continued to deal exclusively in extravagances, flinging intricacies and colossi down aeons of emptiness, heaping profusions of profligacies with ever-fresh vigor. The whole show has been on fire from the word go." [132] Feel that fire, burn with it.

"Scandal of Particularity"

One of the philosophical plagues of our era has been the split between religious institutions, which are deemed holy, and the rest of the world, which is deemed secular. This relegates spiritual experiences to specific places and scheduled times, while leaving us wandering secular deserts the rest of the time.

The challenge becomes finding meaning and spirituality just as we are, where we are. Most of our major religions are based on encounters between man and God that occurred long ago and far away. History did not place us as contemporaries of these religious founders, but instead placed us here today. Annie Dillard in *Pilgrim at Tinker Creek* refers to this mismatch in place and time as "the scandal of particularity." [133] We did not walk the Earth thousands of years ago, when religions were born. If we are to find the door to spirituality, we must find it here and now.

An event can only happen in our world by happening at a particular place and a particular time. Gautama the Buddha, for example, had his moment of enlightenment sitting beside a tree, but it was a specific tree, the now legendary bo tree. For Annie Dillard, Eternity appeared also through a tree, this time a cedar tree that lit up before her eyes. "I saw the backyard cedar where the mourning doves roost charged and transfigured, each cell buzzing with flame. I stood on the grass with the lights in it, grass that was wholly fire, utterly focused and utterly dreamed." [134]

Further along in the book, she states, "I discover that, although the door to the tree with the lights in it was opened from eternity, as it were, and shone on that tree eternal lights, it nevertheless opened on the real and present cedar." [135]

The implication is that today we can only reach the Eternal through the present and the particular. We were not among the Hebrew tribes when Moses is said to have come down from the mountain with his two tablets inscribed in divine fire. Life has been granted to us now, at this moment, in this place. If we are to touch Eternity now, the door must open here. And why not? Why should the Eternal skip this moment or this place?

Jack Kornfield, Buddhist teacher, states, "If you can't find the truth right where you are, where else do you think you will find it?" [136] He offers encouragement: "That which is timeless is found now." [137]

The Eternal must be here, but not as an abstract ideal. It may be found in a tree, a group of letters on a piece of paper, a melody, a kind word, a smile. In a landscape of the apparently mundane, we must be alert for specific moments when the door to Eternity swings open through the true and real forms of the world we inhabit.

Yet, much of our time must be spent earning a living, paying bills, paying taxes. We are not allowed full-time pursuit of the eternal; superficial voices, more tantalizing or urgent, draw our attention. To the extent that we think of the world in terms of whether we are winning or losing the countless battles that we daily wage, our life becomes those battles.

In fact, if we can become aware even occasionally of the divine process that manifests itself in the forms we previously considered commonplace, how might our life change? After all, we cannot live bathed in eternal bliss on mountaintops, but must continue to function in this world. There is an old Eastern saying:

Before Enlightenment
Chopping wood, carrying water.
After Enlightenment
Chopping wood, carrying water.

The tasks that confronted us before still confront us. It is we, ourselves, who are capable of transformation.

Timothy Leary, notorious for his advocacy of hallucinogenic drugs, spoke of the dangers of being caught up in a "reality" in which each step is dictated by the steps that precede it, without thoughtful consideration. What is reality, he asked, and who gets to decide? The daily routine of life can blind us to our own power to make choices. Step back from time to time and make space for yourself, he advised. Look at your world and your life with fresh eyes outside the programmed sequence of your daily routine. Carry with you the insights you gain as you re-enter the everyday life that is yours. [138]

Any given door to Eternity opens and closes in time, sometimes in unexpected fashion. If your heart is open, watching a bird fly or a baby smile can burst open that door for a few precious moments, but that particular door won't stay open forever.

Annie Dillard describes another mystical experience when a mountain lit up for her near sunset, and she felt a sense of enchantment. As soon as she sought to hold on to this moment, the magic vanished. Once the ego became an active participant, trying to hold a moment, the mountain became just another mountain. "I look at the mountain, which is still doing its tricks, as you look at a still-beautiful face belonging to a person who was once your lover in another country years ago: with fond nostalgia, and recognition, but no real feeling save a secret astonishment that you are now strangers." [139]

Have you discovered a door through which the miraculous has cast aside its mundane disguise and revealed itself to you? Just because we cannot always access it, the Eternal does not disappear. Where do you find passion and meaning?

To again quote Dillard: "It never stops. New shows roll in from over the mountains and the magician reappears unannounced from a fold in the curtain you never dreamed was an opening." [140]

"The scandal of particularity" has placed us here and now, and this is where we must seek Eternity. It is as good a place and time as any, if we will only look, listen, and feel. We have been given a world to explore, a succession of potentially transcendent moments, and a physical body as a vehicle of exploration. Doors are opening all around us. To see them, open your mind.

Family Tree

It is time to make a family tree. Start with a big sheet of paper because the list of relatives is longer than you might think. I will follow part of Guy Murchie's outline in the section of *The Seven Mysteries of Life* he entitles "The Interrelatedness of All Creatures." That title might give you a hint of how many relatives you have.

All humans, he tells us, are cousins. "In fact, no human being (of any race) can be less closely related to any other human than approximately fiftieth cousin, and most of us (no matter what color our neighbors) are a lot closer." [141] Presuming humanity began with one or a few common ancestors and then fanned out, ultimate universal relationship among people is undeniable. There were always at least some who crossed racial and ethnic borders in their romantic liaisons, so no group remained reproductively isolated throughout its history. Hence, Murchie states, "It should hardly be necessary now for me to point out that there is no such thing as a pure race, nor any race of men on Earth that is unrelated to other races." [142]

He continues, "And the fact means that your own ancestors, whoever you are, include not only some blacks, some Chinese and some Arabs, but all the blacks, Chinese, Arabs, Malays, Latins, Eskimos and every other possible ancestor who lived on Earth around A.D. 700." [143]

"It is virtually certain therefore that you are a direct descendant of Muhammad and every fertile predecessor of his, including Krishna, Confucius, Abraham, Buddha, Caesar, Ishmail and Judas Iscariot. Of course you must be descended from millions who have lived since Muhammad, inevitably including kings and criminals, but the earlier they lived the more surely you are their descendant." [144]

There are quite a few people to list on the family tree, including everyone on Earth now and an enormous number who lived before, back to the dawn of humanity. The family tree extends even farther back than that. The first human common ancestor was himself descended from pre-existing primates, who were descended from other mammals, and the chain of begets and begets pushes back to the one-celled organisms that gave rise to the evolutionary parade of all animals that followed.

Religions have their stories about how life developed from non-life, and science struggles to explain this miracle, but either way, an original relative of ours was formed from the non-living Earth. Murchie elaborates: "And by this criterion, our quadrillionth cousinhood surely must include the mineral kingdom and even the superorganism of Earth herself with all her elements." [145] The Bible hints at this relationship when it relates that the progenitor of the human race was named Adam, which incorporates the sense of "ground" or "Earth" in its meaning. "Further," Murchie continues, "... by applying celestial genetics from the time Earth's closest ancestor (the Sun) spawned his family of planets and moons, we discover close sidereal cousins among the Milky Way's stars and more distant ones in remoter galaxies and supergalaxies - all these being relatives of estimable propinquity, which, if you can stomach specificity to its ultimate, bring every last one of them within an ordinal compass of cousinhood delineable within about twenty figures." [146] Primack and Abrams go back even farther: "After all, our earliest ancestors, the elementary hydrogen nuclei that came out of the Big Bang, are 10% of our body today, by weight." [147]

Hence you will need to set aside time to list on the family tree every star of every galaxy. More closely, our bodies integrate the chemicals of Earth, the gases of the atmosphere, and the energy from the Sun, so all these must be listed as particularly close relatives. After all, these ingredients compose our very bodies, so our relationship could hardly be closer. Every plant exhales oxygen that we inhale and incorporate into our living self; every animal exhales carbon dioxide to support those plants.

Our family tree fans out to include all organisms living now, all organisms that ever lived. It extends to include Mother Earth herself, from which the original organisms were made, as well as all current organisms. Beyond that, the Earth was formed out of a gas cloud from which the Sun condensed, the same gas cloud from which all stars formed. Everywhere you look, everything you see is engraved on a line of your family tree. Every person you meet is no more remote than a cousin.

It would be easier to make a list of everything that is not related to you. That sheet would be blank.

One Hand Clapping

Perhaps the most famous Zen riddle is, "What is the sound of one hand clapping?" This is, of course, an impossible contradiction, but what might it mean?

A clap is a collision between two things, specifically two hands. A clap may then represent dualism; the loud collision of two opposing hands can be considered a symbol of conflict between two entities. There can only be a conflict, a collision, if two opposing forces exist. Zen and Taoism say everything that exists is a manifestation of a single process, so all apparent conflicts are subsumed in an overarching oneness. If there is only one process, there is nothing to collide with it.

If the world is analogous to the one hand, there is nothing for the world to clap against. If we view our life as a conflict between ourself and the world, our hopes and plans collide with the world frequently. All too often we turn our life into the other hand which collides with the stronger hand of the universe. If we can accept simply being what we are, part of the one hand, that painful collision of man versus world vanishes from our perspective.

The riddle cannot be answered within our conventional worldview. It challenges that worldview by asking whether the second hand is merely an illusion, and warns us not to unnecessarily consider ourselves the illusory second hand that claps against the universe.

Kierkegaard's Prayer

It is said that Danish philosopher Soren Kierkegaard initially prayed in the traditional manner, in a consecrated building (a church). He ultimately gave this method up, deciding that there was nothing he could say that an omniscient deity did not already know. After trying and ultimately rejecting silent prayer, Kierkegaard decided that the most appropriate form of prayer was listening. This then became his spiritual practice. [148] Through this act, Kierkegaard not only turned the concept of prayer inside out, but also converted the entire world into his sanctuary. The chorus of the world is audible everywhere.

If we follow his example, instead of reaching outward to try to contact Divinity, we can be aware of Divinity contacting us. A bird's song becomes more than a bird's song if listening to it becomes a prayer. Hearing leaves rustling in the wind is an act of tuning in to the miracle of the world. The buzzing of bees as they pollinate flowers is part of a symphony that is constantly playing around us, requiring only our attention and receptive heart to turn our world and our backyard into a spiritual place.

Try it now. Walk out into your yard or into a park. Listen as the world contacts you. This is a long-practiced form of meditation, mindfully tuning in to sounds drifting in and out through the flowing stream of time, sounds a world makes to which our ears are attuned. Think of this act as Divinity making itself known to you. You cannot hold on to these sounds any more than you can hold on to time itself as you experience them and let them go, to be replaced by new transient notes in the ongoing melody of our magical world. The melody is ancient but each note is new, and you are here with the ability to listen to the music the Divine plays through the instrument of our world.

Listening is just one of our senses, just one conduit through which our miraculous world makes itself apparent to us. Once the mind is opened, conscious awareness of each taste and touch likewise becomes a form of prayer. How amazing it is that we can taste and touch! Every place becomes a holy place, and every act of awareness has the potential to be a prayer through which you can open yourself to Divinity.

You could just as easily consider your vision to be a form of prayer. The world is artwork that is always in progress, never completed, and you have the gift of vision to watch it unfold. All forms, including the tallest mountains, are transient. You can watch the addition of the newest brushstrokes one moment at a time. Branches sway in the wind, clouds drift, birds fly, squirrels climb. Other changes are slower; grass grows, flowers blossom. You have a front-row seat as this act of ongoing creation penetrates your consciousness through the window of your eyes. Nothing you see exists in isolation; every part is played upon by other parts in a worldwide tapestry.

Observe any transient form as it dances before you; every flower you see open at this moment is a gift from the world to you. How marvelous it is that Divinity reaches out to you through this flower and gives you the eyes and mind that can turn this perception into a prayer. You are a holy being standing in a holy space. Every act of mindfully tasting, touching, seeing, and hearing is a sacred act.

Many people seek fuller lives by purchasing new automobiles or television sets to travel the same old roads and watch the same shows. Some take expensive trips in hopes that distant buildings or oceans might be major upgrades over nearby ones. Few open their ears, eyes, and hearts to the miracle of their own holy spot and their own miraculous self. The Divine is available to you at every waking moment; your body is a vehicle for perceiving it. The world is a very generous place if you choose to accept its gifts. Open your eyes to the canvas of Divinity. Listen to its melody. Taste, smell, touch. Every perception is potentially a prayer, a divine blessing that is yours for the taking.

Skin

As a starting point in thinking about our body, consider the skin that encloses us. A friend of mine - a dermatologist - boasts that skin is the largest organ of the human body. He makes his living treating its imperfections like acne and poison ivy. It is easy to think of the skin in terms of its flaws.

Everyone is aware of its primary function of keeping our insides inside and holding the outside world outside, but skin is much more talented than that. Infants start with just enough skin to enclose their 7-pound bodies. Over the decades as our bodies grow, we don't have to keep shedding small old shells, like lobsters, to grow larger new shells to allow for growth. Instead skin expands to remain a perfectly tailored fit as our body's external garment. It is to a large extent water resistant, in that raindrops and lake water roll off our surface without being absorbed. Unlike other garments, skin re-knits itself when it is torn, serving as a barrier to toxins and infections.

As our interface with the outside world, our skin is loaded with sensors that continually update us about the environment in which we are immersed. Skin is a thermometer with temperature sensors, a threat indicator with pain sensors (and all threats that have reached our skin are potentially urgent!), a pleasure sensor, and a reliable indicator about orientation in space. Nerves act as couriers transmitting data from skin receptors to the brain, where command decisions are made. Your entire skin surface is an advanced monitoring system, designed for your safety, sending continual updates from your border.

Unlike a wool coat, skin changes its thermal properties based on whether the body needs to release or retain heat. In the cold of winter, muscles associated with the skin generate shivering and "goose bumps;" this muscle activity produces heat and thereby warms us. During torrid summer, skin pores open and sweat glands release fluid (perspiration) whose evaporation provides cooling.

Of course, when we see each other, it is the outer surface that we view, making the cosmetic features of skin an important means by which people superficially judge each other. "Skin deep" becomes a metaphor for superficiality. Different cultures have their own unique standards by which the beauty of skin is assessed. Alas, such superficial assessments are often driven by perceived flaws.

You have been given an external covering that changes shape with you, shields you from many outside threats, and provides continual updates about your surroundings. Old skin is continually being shed at its outer surface and replaced by new growth from underneath over the course of weeks. You have been given quite a remarkable garment. With all its versatility, it will last you a lifetime.

The Miracle of You

Beneath the outer covering of the skin, consider what is happening. There is no starting point in describing how a human body works. The body contains interwoven processes that are useless on their own, yet integral to the workings of the whole. Any choice of where to jump into the saga of our biology is arbitrary, and there is no stopping point while we still live. Wheels continue to turn other wheels, each essential to the whole assemblage. The story need not even start by describing what happens within us, for we could just as easily begin with the origin of the gases we breathe, the foods that we eat, or the ancestors whose mating choices resulted eventually in the unique DNA sequences in our cells.

Without astronomical events that generated oxygen, our lungs would be useless. Without lungs to draw in oxygen, and a digestive tract to collect nutrients from the outside world, our brain and heart would be rendered non-functional. Without a heart to pump blood, or kidneys to detoxify it, other organs would fail. Our bodies require a steady supply of additives from the outside to enable our internal systems to support each other.

We could, for example, consider our physical structure. Our calcium-rich bony skeleton holds our shape and anchors our muscles, while the marrow of our bones synthesizes our blood cells. The calcium now nestling in our bones and teeth was created in stellar explosions in distant parts of the galaxy. That calcium, after drifting through space, became part of Earth's crust, and emerged within the living bodies of plants. Perhaps that calcium became part of you after grazing cattle incorporated it into milk that reached your refrigerator.

Stellar explosions are likewise the source of the oxygen and iron that currently waltz together through your blood vessels. The iron became part of the Earth's crust, from which it was drawn into plants such as spinach or beans, and further concentrated within animals that ate the plants. Through your diet, this trans-galactic element entered you. No mere tourist, the iron was put to work as the agent by which hemoglobin not only transports oxygen via blood circulation to your trillions of cells, but releases it at the proper address.

Or - as another arbitrary starting point in telling our story - we could consider what happens when we expand our chest wall, allowing the air molecules within our lungs to spread out. This lowers the pressure within the lungs compared to the pressure of the atmospheric air outside, and this lowered pressure draws the atmosphere into our airways. The outside air enters our chest, spreads out through the lung's air pockets, and its oxygen is extracted. The oxygen traverses across thin membranes into blood vessels and into the waiting embrace of hemoglobin for its journey through our arteries.

All this would be worthless if we did not have a delivery system capable of effectively circulating our cosmic chemicals. Indeed, we possess a heart that spontaneously beats about 100,000 times each day, pumping blood through a system of enclosed vessels estimated at about *50,000 miles* in collective length. Can you even imagine thousands of miles of blood vessels - most of that length in a vast number of tiny, narrow capillaries - in a body your size? All your trillions of cells are dependent on nearby capillaries, through which fresh supplies are transported to the cell and wastes carted off. The heart relies on our internal sensors to set its rate and workload, automatically tailoring its function to our situation.

When you go for your daily jog, for example, your heart increases both its pace and the volume of blood delivered with each beat. When you sleep, it relaxes.

As the blood delivers oxygen, it collects toxins and metabolic by-products such as carbon dioxide for eventual removal. Kidneys retain the good stuff and excrete the rest. Lungs exhale back into the atmosphere the carbon dioxide that likely will quickly be taken in by plants, where those molecules will become part of another living being.

Certainly for purposes of being human, it is obvious that a physical body provides the vehicle for our existence, so perhaps we might start our tale by considering how we build a body. DNA lines up atoms, but we must acquire most of those atoms via the process of digestion (the rest, of course, we inhale from the atmosphere). Though we may be 5 or 6 feet tall, we find room for a 30-foot-long digestive tract that contains enhancements. In the small intestine, millions of tiny projections called villi branch into microvilli, increasing the absorptive surface area by a factor of 30- to 60-fold. With our sense of taste dictating our dietary choices and stomach acid minimizing the entry of germs, we rely on our intestines to absorb the nutrients and water from which we are made.

Think about everything you eat, all the pizza and popcorn, and realize that the body you construct with those ingredients does not look at all like pizza or popcorn. Your digestive tract breaks the foods you eat down to tiny components, the building blocks that make up fats, proteins, and carbohydrates. These are absorbed into blood vessels within the intestinal wall and delivered to the tissues of your body. Depending on your metabolic needs at the time, the nutrients are directed to that purpose. Just as a wooden shed can be broken down into individual boards that can be used to make a new structure, the digestive tract reduces our food into its basic subunits, which our body utilizes to make and sustain itself.

As the blood totes the newly digested nutrients around, the liver grabs some to make liver tissue, and the heart grabs some to make heart. It is like a buffet in which the body's organs absorb what they need to refurbish themselves.

However, the body's organization can hardly be described as "every cell for itself;" there are managers all over the place. Glands that secrete hormones oversee certain domains under their charge. The ovaries and testes secrete sexual hormones, the adrenal glands synthesize numerous metabolically vital hormones like adrenaline, and the thyroid's hormone sets our metabolic rate. These glands serve only as middle management, under the auspices of the so-called master gland, the pituitary. The pituitary in turn receives orders from the brain's hypothalamus, providing our body with multiple levels of managerial control. Yet none of these managers is given a free hand; all are part of feedback loops in which the products of the system regulate the behavior of the managers. When the body functions properly, if a chemical (like sodium) or hormone (like adrenaline) becomes too high or low, higher levels of management in the body's regulatory hierarchy activate mechanisms that restore normality. The wonder of our bodies is not merely found in the interweaving of its processes, but also the precision of its control.

Should infection come our way, we are defended by an immune system that identifies and eliminates the intruder. Should our tissues be damaged, they often repair themselves. Out of the barrage of stimuli that impinge upon us, our senses allow us to identify the information we need to survive.

Our brain could not exist without a body to support it and an environment in which the body can survive. Yet the brain is a physical structure, part of the weave, but somehow able to knit intangible thoughts from a collection of atoms. As we direct those thoughts toward exploring the nature of ourselves, it does not matter which point of entry we choose. All lead to the whole, the intertwined collection of processes through which protons, neutrons, and electrons spring to life and experience the world.

We have grown up looking at our self through the wrong end of the telescope, shrinking our self-image. Consider any aspect of your amazing body, your set of interactions with a universe that lives and thinks through you. Think of the opportunity the next moment affords, the opportunity to truly experience being what you are in a universe like this one. Then simply be yourself.

What Makes Us Human?

What makes humans human? Our physical feats are hardly impressive within the animal kingdom. Cheetahs can run three times as fast as our fastest sprinters, and kangaroos can outleap our Olympic champions. Relative to their size, ants can outlift our bodybuilding champs and grasshoppers can spring 20 times their own height, trouncing our pole vaulters. We are bigger than most animals, but could hardly survive on our athleticism alone. As for reproductive superiority, our one-at-a-time birth rate after nine months' gestation ranks us near the bottom of nature's breeders.

We can't swim like fish, but we can construct boats and submarines. We can't fly like birds, but we can outrace them if we use a rocket. Monkeys have dexterous hands that allow them to swing gracefully through the branches of tropical jungles. Our opposable thumbs, definitely a hindrance to tree-swinging, are quite useful for making and utilizing tools.

Although we have very fancy internal organs that are excellent at their jobs, other mammals use a similar internal setup. They use lungs for oxygen intake, hearts to pump the oxygen through blood vessels to the tissues of the body, mouths to ingest fluids and food at the upper terminus of well-functioning digestive tracts for nutrient absorption. All have effective kidneys for modulating body chemistry (including camels, which utilize world-class kidneys for journeys across vast deserts). These other mammals have vertebrae similar to ours that anchor bony skeletons with ribs and a pelvis and four extremities, and muscles eerily similar to our own. We and our fellow mammals share variants of the same basic body plan. A cow has a liver, a monkey has a liver, and so do we.

We share one additional fascinating feature with other animals and plants - we are all inhabited. Each of us is actually an ecosystem rather than a solitary being. It is estimated that our own body contains about 10 times as many bacterial cells as human ones. Bacteria reside on our skin and in our digestive tract, plus numerous other niches, and contribute several pounds to our weight. In general these bacteria cause us no problems, and many may actually be protective, particularly in the digestive tract, where they ward off potentially dangerous bacteria.

Of particular interest are the mitochondria within each of our cells. Mitochondria are a type of "organelle," a term that refers to subunits within individual cells. Many people are aware that our mitochondria are the powerhouses that generate energy within our body, allowing us for example to walk across the room. Passed from a mother to her offspring within the egg that is fertilized by sperm, mitochondria that are genetically the same as those within our mother's cells are now within every one of our cells, acting as miniature batteries. Despite all the brilliance of our other interwoven organ systems, we would be inert without our mitochondria.

Research by Lynn Margulis in the 1970s and by others since provides strong evidence that mitochondria in the early days of life on Earth were once free-living bacteria. Swallowed up by larger one-celled organisms, mitochondria were not digested but rather developed a symbiotic relationship with the organisms in which they began to dwell. [149] The host provided a safe haven, while the mitochondria returned the favor by providing energy. So successful was this union that as host organisms evolved to become complex and multicellular, each organism continued to house mini-power-plant mitochondria in all of its cells. The DNA within mitochondria is similar to bacterial DNA and different from human DNA. Therefore, all our cells contain the human DNA that we inherited from each parent, plus living mitochondria with their own DNA that is the same in all the mitochondria in our body, a gift from our mother. Mitochondria even reproduce within our cells independent of our own cellular reproduction. We are hybrids.

Speaking of mitochondria, physician and author Lewis Thomas writes, "They are much less closely related to me than to each other and to the free-living bacteria out under the hill. They feel like strangers, but the thought comes that the same creatures, precisely the same, are out there in the cells of seagulls, and whales, and dune grass, and seaweed, and hermit crabs, and further inland in the leaves of the beech in my backyard and in the family of skunks beneath the back fence, and even in that fly on the window.

Through them, I am connected; I have close relatives, once removed, all over the place." [150]

It is likewise presumed that the power source for green plants, the chloroplasts that capture sunlight for photosynthesis on which our entire ecosystem is based, were also once independently living organisms. Presumably ingested by the one-celled forerunners to modern plants, chloroplasts are now present in every cell within the leaves of green plants, again offering energy in return for a stable home. These interlopers not only make possible the plant life on which animals dine, but also via photosynthesis churn out the oxygen that animals breathe. Again quoting Thomas, "It is a good thing for the entire enterprise that mitochondria and chloroplasts have remained small, conservative, and stable, since these two organelles are, in a fundamental sense, the most important living things on earth. Between them they produce the oxygen and arrange for its use. In effect, they run the place." [151]

Despite all the amazing interacting systems that keep us alive, we would be little more than doormats if we did not have those aliens in our cells. David Suzuki summarizes, "Thus, each of us is a community of organisms. We are each an aggregate of trillions of cells, every one of which is inhabited by numerous descendents of parasites; they now provide services for us in return for an ecological niche." [152]

Although the effective interplay of remarkable internal systems - and intracellular alien organisms - allows the survival of all multicellular organisms, it is clearly the human brain that distinguishes us as a species. Presumably there exists a gradation in mental function as evolution crafts larger and more complex brains. An earthworm that eats dirt, chemically modifies it internally, and then excretes it is unlikely to ask what life is all about. For that earthworm, untouched by existential angst, life is basically, "Dirt in, dirt out." We humans enjoy the richness of far greater complexity and creativity, but are also left with far deeper questions.

The development of complex language to formulate and communicate ideas requires a brain that can code and decode symbols, such as letters and words, plus the physical structures that generate the symbols. These include the larynx, lips, tongue, and teeth to produce spoken language and ears to perceive it. While every birdsong and cricket chirp is clearly a communication, our human brains allow us to explore a universe of ideas not accessible to other species. With a finite number of letters and sounds, we generate dictionaries full of words that can be woven into an infinite number of combinations. Ideas transmitted via human language lead to shared knowledge and more advanced concepts in a steady and unending feedback. We do not face the next moment at square zero on the knowledge scale, but have access as a species to a vast array of stored human knowledge.

For much of human history, "mind" was considered an entity whose relationship to the brain was uncertain, if such a relationship existed at all. Modern technology tightens the link between the two, but deep mysteries persist. Current research demonstrates that regions of the brain are active in reproducible patterns as we generate and experience thoughts and emotions. As we shall soon explore, a physical mechanism appears to be at work, though no one appears close to understanding that mechanism.

Our wondrous brain comes equipped with a vast array of accessible programs, allowing us to quickly change mental channels. It is linked to a sensory network through which a continuous input from the outside world provides moment-to-moment updates. The brain is further hooked up to neuromuscular relays through which we are capable of a wide range of responses, including an integrated vocal system that allows us to bridge the gap with other humans.

We also use the brain to explore itself, seeking clues to the roots of our own identity. Each advance raises deeper questions, more questions. Obviously there are limits to what we can learn when our mind is the tool that seeks to understand itself. What we as explorers are capable of comprehending limits what we can ultimately discover. Still, it is fascinating to wade into the mystery.

Mind and Brain

The relationship between mind and brain has been difficult to pin down because both sides of the debate seem so implausible. Can mind exist apart from brain? On the one hand, we have no idea how a physical 3-pound brain can generate non-physical thoughts, as well as create an inner representation of the universe. On the other hand, we don't find conscious minds wandering loose outside living bodies. We are at the very dawn of scientific exploration of this fascinating puzzle, long the subject of philosophers and theologians.

Electroencephalograms (EEGs) for decades have detected via electrodes placed on the scalp that electrical activity within the brain varies during different states of consciousness, with typical patterns for sleep and alert wakefulness, for example. This has been a relatively insensitive approach to our mind-brain question, partly because EEGs detect only a small number of wave patterns, nothing commensurate with the enormous complexity of brain functions.

The most sensitive current method of studying the brain in action is the functional magnetic resonance imaging scan (fMRI). MRIs use the magnetic properties of atoms in response to magnetic fields generated during the scan to take detailed radiological pictures of the structure being studied, in this case, the brain. The functional aspect is assessed by observing changes in the rate of metabolism, typically the rate of oxygen consumption, as the brain performs its tricks. When a brain region strongly increases its rate of metabolic activity, that brain area is presumed to be actively involved in the cerebral task being studied.

Different modes of thought cause specific parts of the physical brain to light up on functional MRIs. The possibility that mind could exist independently from brain seems unlikely when areas of the brain are activated with each mental process. Perform mental mathematics, utilize language centers to organize sentences, meditate, contemplate Divinity, experience strong emotions - all of these disparate types of thinking activate reproducible patterns within the brain.

No two brains are exactly the same, though individual differences are superimposed on underlying similarities in brain organization. In general, the left side of the brain is more involved in detail recognition, complex planning for the future, and language, while the right side experiences the world more holistically within the context of the present moment, non-verbally.

There are brain centers that evaluate vision, that trigger movement of particular parts of the body, that formulate and comprehend symbols (such as words), that are involved in experiencing emotions. There are combinations of brain areas involved in every function of mind studied so far, from calculating to praying to falling in love. Functional MRI scanning creates an "action shot" of the brain during these processes, revealing the localization and the teamwork of specific brain areas that increase activity as a person goes through the repertoire of mental functions.

There are people who are philosophically troubled by the idea that all the intricacies of mind are "just" manifestations of electrochemical processes within the brain. I put the word "just" in quotation marks because this argument hinges on whether a mind with a physical basis is in some way of lower value than a mind that performs the exact same functions as an entity independent of the body. If the mind is the source of our remarkable reasoning skills and emotion, those thoughts and emotions are certainly just as intense and powerful regardless of their source.

Dr. Jeanette Norden, professor of neuroscience at Vanderbilt University School of Medicine, asks, "Is there any reason to think that just because a strong emotional attachment like 'love' has biological and biochemical correlates in the brain - that it is any less important in human existence?" [153] Certainly, when a person during a functional MRI scan thinks of a loved one and experiences the passion of that love, localized areas of the brain light up on the scan. Physical processes are obviously taking place within the brain concurrent with the psychological experience of love. The mind's bag of tricks is just as spectacular, and the experiences just as "real," when it is recognized that electrochemical brain processes are at work in their generation. In fact, those thoughts and emotions exist *because* the brain has the electrochemical circuitry to manifest them.

You are the one who possesses that brain, with its 100 billion neurons and 100 trillion interconnections. Within your own head sits this powerful tool to comprehend your interaction with the universe. The mechanism of action of the brain remains in many ways unknown and perhaps, to a large extent, unknowable. Still, the brain is yours, with all its complexity, and somehow you already know how to use it. Let us consider what is known about how it works.

Brain

The brain is constructed in a way that has generated every mood or thought we have ever had, though it is unknown how the physical brain produces a single intangible idea. However, we use our brain casually and often effortlessly to perform amazing tasks, such as encoding and decoding spoken and written language, forming interpersonal relationships, spatially navigating across a planet, and in general responding appropriately to the enormous range of experiences the world throws our way.

Our brain is organized into modules, often composed of submodules containing other sets of still smaller submodules. No one knows what the "seat of consciousness" is, whether it is a particular physical (anatomical) place within the brain or a functional coalition among different brain regions, but somehow the brain must match modules or combinations of modules to the current situation that the world presents. You have modules that allow deep reflective thought and rational analysis, modules that generate positive and negative emotions, modules that encode or scan memories, modules that generate or suppress a sense of urgency, modules battling with each other to force their way into our consciousness. Dozens of major modules compete or form alliances, and whichever consortium gains the upper hand will influence how you mentally and emotionally interact with the world. Your mode of response to outside stimuli or your own internal thoughts is contingent on the combination of brain modules that have been activated and the forcefulness of that activation.

This means that you do not have a single, stable personality (perhaps you have noticed that), but flip from the influence of one coalition of modules to another as the experiences of living in a changing world impact you. In describing the struggle for dominance of modules within the brain, acclaimed science writer Steven Johnson writes, "It's a jungle in there." [154]

Each of the brain's modules contains vast numbers of neurons. The communication between neurons is via chemicals called neurotransmitters. Even in the brain, where 100 billion neurons are packed into the relatively small space within the skull, no two neurons touch each other. Between any neuron and the next neuron in a sequence lies a small gap called a synapse. For a neuron to communicate with adjacent neurons, the first neuron must release a neurotransmitter that drifts across the synapse to attach to specific receptors on the next neuron (or neurons) in the sequence. Each brain neuron might receive input from a thousand other neurons, some pelting it with stimulating neurotransmitters while others are flooding it with suppressive ones. If the stimulatory input is sufficiently greater than the inhibitory input, the neuron fires off to eventually release neurotransmitters of its own to activate the next neurons in the chain.

When you experience a change of mode in brain operation, it is not because you acquire a different brain or suffer from "multiple personality disorder." Rather, it is the result of an outpouring of neurotransmitters that suddenly turn on some brain modules and turn off others. About 60 neurotransmitters have been identified to this point. Perhaps you are driving along pleasantly in your car, feeling like the most affable of humans, when another driver recklessly crosses your path. Gone are the soothing thoughts that were drifting through your mind as you enjoyed the song on the car radio. Instead, stress-induced neurotransmitters begin surging through your amygdala, an almond-size brain area that is the trigger point of many emotions, especially fear. As the threat resolves and you realize you are safe, fear melts into anger, and ultimately into relief, as neurotransmitters hijack your equanimity and eventually release you.

Our brain is therefore composed of multiple distinct functional modules, plus the neurotransmitters that allow each module to function. Further, neurotransmitters provide the means by which the brain shifts modules, allowing us to mentally engage the world in so many different ways. Specific modules or combinations of modules battle to capture consciousness, but competition and cooperation between modules also takes place beneath the level of consciousness. Our brain is a chemical cauldron, a sea of waxing and waning neurotransmitters that each have their domain of action. Over the next few pages, I suggest you allow the general sense of the brain's versatility to flow over you, without getting bogged down in the details.

One neurotransmitter much in the news is called oxytocin, nicknamed "the love molecule." Secreted by the brain's hypothalamus, oxytocin is released by nursing mothers and during sexual orgasm, as well as other experiences of deep personal bonding. That is, a module or combination of modules exists, with neurotransmitters that provide the on-off switch and the "intensity switch," to facilitate the experience of love.

The amygdala stands guard over our self-defense. When it is stimulated and triggers the emotion of fear, our rational brain modules buckle under and give way. Self-preservation for any organism requires that other brain centers yield when the amygdala cries out, "Danger!" Think about that - part of the brain specializes in screening the outside world for threats, and its shout of potential danger overrides all other modules like a fire alarm.

Dopamine is a neurotransmitter involved in multiple brain modules. Failure of dopamine in networks involved in neuromuscular control causes Parkinson's disease, which results in a complex of symptoms including tremors and difficulty initiating voluntary movements. In the limbic system of the brain, which plays an important role in memory and emotion, dopamine is a key neurotransmitter in some circuits involved in the behavior of "seeking," defined in this context as wanting what you don't have.

One speculation is that dopamine circuits compare our expectations for an experience with the results we receive. If our expectations are not met, dopamine is involved in our sense of disappointment. It can drive us toward further seeking, even when we rationally recognize that we are not deprived. Dopamine circuits appear to be the culprit in both biological and behavioral addictions. In 2007, Dr. Norden reported that a dopamine pathway between two little publicized brain regions, the ventral tegmental area and the nucleus accumbens septi, was implicated in all known cases of chemical or behavioral addiction. [155]

To pick a simple example of brain organization, the visual system represents one functional module. Light shining on the eye triggers the brain's vision module. Parts of that module are anatomically contiguous at the back of the brain, but some 30 brain regions are involved in creating and interpreting visual images. All such regions are connected by nerves, though not all are structurally adjacent to each other. Perhaps that vision module is the centerpiece of your consciousness as you gaze at a scenic mountain vista or a flower, or perhaps the module works in concert with the language module as you read a book.

In addition, other brain modules may contribute an emotional dimension to the experience, perhaps a sense of satisfaction or joy. The brain's limbic system contains an "endogenous reward system," including the aforementioned ventral tegmental area and nucleus accumbens, as well as parts of the cerebral cortex. If a life experience stimulates the endogenous reward system, neurotransmitters such as dopamine, oxytocin, norepinephrine, and even opioids (chemicals internally produced by the brain that act like opiates) are released. The vision module in the above example has been activated in concert with the endogenous reward system, coating the visual experience with an overlay of happiness. Modules that might otherwise have generated anxiety have been suppressed. It seems like a unified cohesive experience to which you have generated a single simple response, but this tip-of-the-iceberg awareness represents the expression of a deeper complex interplay of specialized brain regions.

Much credit for the ascendancy of the human species has been attributed to the gray matter of the cerebral cortex, whose nerve cells allow the superior rational thought and analytic skills on which our species prides itself. We have been blessed with a large cortex compared with other species, though the nerve cell bodies within the gray matter are confined to a thin strip only 2-4 millimeters wide (about one-eighth of an inch) along the outer edge of the cortex. As if to maximize the amount of gray matter, the brain has many folds to increase the area of its border, and therefore the amount of gray matter and brain cells that can fit along its outer edge. Different parts of the cortex have different specialized functions and belong to different modules, though all parts of the brain are interconnected by a network of nerves.

The limbic system is located more centrally in the brain, and its function is critical to memory and emotion. Although memories appear to primarily be stored in the cerebral cortex, the limbic system's hippocampus is the gateway to the encoding of new memories. Without a functioning hippocampus, a person still has mental access to old, previously encoded memories, but cannot form new ones. This is part of the tragedy of Alzheimer's disease.

The amygdala, as previously mentioned, is critical to generating our emotions, which are of enormous importance in the workings of our mind. We are more likely to remember experiences to which strong emotions are attached. It is our amygdala that, in the words of Steven Johnson, "... somehow marks memories created by other parts of the brain as being emotionally significant..... You can think of this selectivity as the brain's way of underlining." [156] When those memories come back to us, the original emotions tend to come back as well.

Further, although we think of ourselves as people who make decisions rationally, emotions play a huge role. Often decisions are made quickly on an emotional level, after which the rational mind tries to create logical reasons to justify the decision. Dr. Norden discusses a patient named Elliot who, after brain tumor surgery, lost his perception of emotion. Without the backdrop of emotions, Elliot could no longer make decisions. He could come up with rational reasons for or against a particular choice, but,

"Without emotions, he could not weigh the various options." Dr. Norden continues, "... a new paradigm has emerged, one which acknowledges that our 'feelings' play a major role in our ability to make 'rational' judgments.... Without emotions, we, like the patient Elliot, cannot act in our own best interest." [157] It is through the calculus of our emotions, often at a subconscious level, that we personalize the factors involved in a decision, and then make choices that we deem "rational." Thus emotions not only play an important role in how we feel about our experiences, but also largely determine what we remember and how we make decisions. In the words of Dr. Jill Bolte Taylor, a Harvard neuroanatomist and recovered stroke victim, "Although many of us may think of ourselves as thinking creatures that feel, biologically we are feeling creatures that think." [158] In terms of specialized modules, Dr. Norden reports that an area of the cerebral cortex called the orbitofrontal cortex is involved in the inculcation of cultural mores. Hooked into the reward network within the limbic system, the orbitofrontal cortex provides an individual with positive emotional feedback for following cultural mores, regardless of the culture to which he or she belongs. [159] The evening news, filled with stories about fanatical followers of apparently crazed leaders, becomes less bewildering when one realizes that the brain is pre-programmed to adapt the beliefs and behaviors of one's culture.

In more general terms, the brain contains modules that not only perform specific functions, but also modules that stamp such experiences with particular emotions that encourage or discourage related behaviors. To further quote Steven Johnson, "The brain contains chemicals that create pleasure and reward; it also contains chemicals that create the appetite for pleasure and reward." [160] Dopamine is felt to play an important role in generating such appetites.

Our brain provides many different combinations of modules that allow us to match responses to a constantly changing world. Part of successful survival requires having functionally effective modules, and part requires the ability to quickly shift to an appropriate set of modules that matches the challenges of the moment. Like a football team that must counter an opponent by utilizing an effective combination of players, the brain must address each life situation by bringing forth an appropriate combination of modules. Happiness researchers Ed Diener and Robert Biswas-Diener's observation, "... that most people are mildly happy most of the time ..." is likely due to our baseline balance of modules and neurotransmitters. [161]

Part of the learning process of life requires identifying which of our modules are our strengths and which experiences activate our brain's endogenous reward system. We must also learn what triggers our amygdala's anxiety response and evaluate appropriately whether such perceived threats are real.

All the while, the brain is awash in a shifting blend of neurotransmitters. All external drugs or chemicals that affect the brain do so by impacting neurotransmitters. Taking an aspirin for a headache is effective because it alters neurotransmitters involved in the brain's perception of pain.

Opiates such as morphine and codeine affect the brain because the brain, under routine operating conditions, secretes opiate-like chemicals called endorphins and enkephalins, which have their own specific receptors in the brain. Endorphins and enkephalins are thought to provide us with natural relief from both physical and psychological pain. It is to these receptors that synthetic opiates bind, after which they are processed in a manner similar to the body's own enkephalins and endorphins. Johnson states, "... the fundamental truth is that artificial drugs work because your brain mistakes them for natural ones. Right now, as you read these words, you are under the influence of chemicals that are, molecularly speaking, almost indistinguishable from drugs that could get you arrested if you consume them openly in a public place." [162] He continues, "So begin with this basic premise: you are on drugs. With every shifting mood, every twitch of anxiety, every lovelorn glance, you are experiencing the release of dedicated chemicals in your brain that control your emotions...." [163]

Johnson includes a cautionary note. When the brain synthesizes and releases chemicals, it has internal controls that limit the process. Recreational drug use can flood the system with dangerously high levels of these chemicals, potentially resulting in brain damage or even fatal overdose as high chemical concentrations overwhelm the brain's ability to metabolize and clear the drug. [164]

The brain is, of course, part of a physical body, which sets the environment in which the brain functions. The body's state of rest or exhaustion, health or illness, hormone status, and, of course, stress level, all play a huge role in the brain's inner workings. All of our activities and experiences influence the brain, affect the release and metabolism of neurotransmitters, and alter the consortium of modules that gain control of the mysterious "seat of consciousness." Behind the scenes, subconscious processes influence conscious ones, as we find ourselves suddenly aware of opinions or ideas that seemingly emerge out of nowhere. Where do ideas come from?

Again, we are left with a great mystery. Without an understanding of the brain's internal workings, we construct a personalized User's Manual. Despite a similar general plan, no two brains are the same, and every brain is modified by each life event. In the process we call learning, new brain hookups are constantly being formed by our experiences, uniquely tailoring our brain to the life we live. Each hookup we create in our brain today increases the power of the "antenna" with which we attract further knowledge and meaning from our future experiences. Each day we build connections that will be part of our future brain.

In addition to a set of modules that allow us through our senses to perceive the outside world, we also come equipped with additional modules that allow us to interpret those experiences, to paint them with emotion, and to learn from them. We can even turn our attention inward and deepen our self-knowledge. Part of that process should include an awareness of our casual brilliance in effortlessly and appropriately shifting brain modules in our lifelong dance with the world.

It seems to me unlikely, outside of horror movies, that any hypothetical disembodied minds exist. They would be subject to a major logistics problem, namely, how would they obtain their information? In horror movies, those fiendish brains in bubbling containers can typically see and hear, for example, in the absence of eyes and ears. Bodies offer a significant advantage; they provide input through an organism's senses, allowing it to monitor its environment, both internal and external. Our brain, with all its modules, is bathed with steady streams of sensory data, for which our body proves indispensable. Further, when brains respond to incoming signals, bodies provide the mechanism for response.

For a brain to be effective, regardless of its intrinsic capabilities, it requires adequate input and the means to react effectively within an appropriate time frame. Computer networks are reshaping the debate not only about what constitutes intelligence, but also about whether technological entities of the future can in some way embody properties we now associate with life.

But what about us, with our customary brain-within-body arrangement? Clearly we are spectacularly alive, so our senses must have provided data essential for survival, and our brains must have processed the information quickly and accurately. Much of the experience of being human exists in the interplay between the sensory channels through which the world interacts with us and the makeup of our brain that interprets the experience. Is grass really green? Is the drumbeat loud? Does the experience make us happy?

Eyewitness

"I saw it with my own eyes." A so-called "eyewitness" might say this if he's certain of the truth of his vision as a first-hand observer. We likewise accept as true our other sensory experiences - smell, taste, hearing, touch. All this presumes that truth exists "out there," and that through our senses, we gain access to this truth. If we experience it ourselves, we know it is true.

Yet, though our senses are marvelous tools for survival and therefore must convey a core of true information, they also alter and skew all transmissions. We see what we need to see to survive, for example, but the objects of the outside world are unlikely to exist in the colors they appear to us. Our sense of hearing, more formally known as audition, detects vibrations. It is uncertain whether sound exists at all in the outside world or is merely a construct in the perceptions of a listener whose auditory tract turns external vibrations into the subjective experience of sound.

Any organism's sense of taste and smell must draw it toward safe behaviors and away from dangerous ones. Each species has its own dietary requirements - it must be lured to ingest nutritious items and shun toxic ones. The sense of taste must motivate an animal to eat what it requires to survive. Birds, as an example, consider a buffet of worms and insects the height of dining pleasure.

Further, the brain must not be overwhelmed by the many incoming data streams. It must be able to identify urgent information and consign the rest to a mental wastebasket of ignored signals. An effective brain requires a skillful editor.

Hence, we are not detectives walking through a world in which internal senses accurately report external truths. Each sense is tailored toward enhancing our survival by providing biased perceptions through which our conceptualizations emerge. All our sensory experiences contain truth wrapped in bias.

Through our interpretation of sensory data, we are also defining our relationship with the world. The traditional interpretation has been that we are skin-enclosed beings to whom sensory channels disclose external reality. If, however, the nature of the outside world and *our own* nature are both partially discoverable through the interactions provided by our sensory experiences, then those interactions shed equal light on the world outside and the world within, which are all manifestations of the same world. When we see a cat jump over a fence, we learn not only about the cat's dexterity, but also that we are equipped with neurological mechanisms to encode the experience visually and integrate the observation into our conceptualization of cats and fences, eyes and minds.

What Is Truth?

One of the unanswerable questions about the world is the extent to which it is knowable by living organisms. We feel we can understand much about life because of the ease with which we see the world, hear it, smell it, taste it, touch it. Our sensory experiences seem so direct and obvious that we take for granted that they must be true, that the world must exist in the way we perceive it. Yet in discovering the mechanisms by which our senses present the world to us, we also learn some of the creative bias our sensory systems interject into the drama of our life. We *do not perceive the world as it is, but in a manner that enhances our survival.* To thoughtfully consider a single glance out the window or a single spoken word takes us on a journey more mysterious than a rocket traveling to a distant planet.

Every species of animal needs a combination of sensors to allow its survival, based on the demands of its lifestyle. Although our own species now supplements its sensory information with technological data from devices such as telescopes and microscopes, through most of human history we had to make do with the "outside world detection kit" provided by our own body.

Sensory experiences do not merely provide insight into the processes of the outside world - they also come shaded with overtones of pleasure and discomfort that drive our behavior. If a rabbit of ancient times perceived eating strychnine as pleasurable, such toxic dining killed it off, and it did not beget future generations of strychnine lovers. If an otherwise similar rabbit found toxic substances distasteful and nutritious food such as a carrot delicious, and responded by eating food it found delicious while avoiding the distasteful, it survived and thrived by following its tastes. The surviving rabbit passed down genes resulting in offspring that were attracted by taste to the same nutritious carrots, while shunning toxic strychnine. It is not the truth that carrots are universally delicious to all organisms; instead, those rabbits that find carrots delicious are more likely to survive and pass down that genetic predisposition, resulting in a carrot-loving rabbit species today.

Over countless generations, dangerous encounters with the environment tended to become associated with negative sensory experiences, such as pain or an unpleasant smell or taste. The genetic predisposition to avoid such negative sensory interactions led to safer behaviors and ultimately more offspring that shared the same protective genetic endowment. Many activities that promote survival and reproduction (such as eating or sexual intercourse) became associated with powerful positive sensory experiences. Often these behavioral predispositions became genetically encoded as instincts. Senses do not merely provide data, but also push and pull an animal's behavior toward improved survival.

We can appreciate our own sensory interactions from the inside. Our brain, operation headquarters, is housed within the protective armor of our skull, where it is to some extent shielded from the outside world. This presents the problem of getting information to and from the brain. We, like other animals, establish sensory front lines along our periphery manned by specialized tissues that are sensitive to processes by which the outside world impinges upon us. These receptors provide the channels through which the world becomes knowable. Nerves then serve as couriers relaying information from receptors on the periphery of our body to the brain. It is generally said that we have five major sensory channels, far fewer channels than a television set.

Yet this five-pack of senses working in combination has allowed the survival of millions of animal species, though some species have additional senses such as the perception of magnetic fields. All animals, for example, need a way to monitor their border with the outside world, and therefore require a sense of touch. Deployed in and near our skin, acting as patrols stationed on the boundary between the outside universe and what we call our "self," are tactile receptors stimulated by direct physical contact. Similar receptors are also located within our body, notifying us when our stomach is overly distended after that second dessert, or when our knees and feet are achy after too many steps. Thus the sense of touch, or more formally the "somatosensory system," monitors our border and our interior.

We also have "energy detectors" that give us knowledge of more distant aspects of the environment. Through vision, we utilize receptors within our eyes to obtain critical data via light that has reflected off objects in the outside world and into our retinas. With our ears we learn about the world through its vibrations.

We also have "chemical detection kits" in our noses and mouths, providing us with the ability to smell and taste. If something smells bad, it is wise to avoid it. The senses of taste and smell combine to advise us whether or not to take an external substance into our body as food or drink. A bitter taste warned our distant ancestors against ingesting potentially toxic chemicals, enabling them to live and procreate, so we should likewise be warned by such a taste.

Structurally, a sensory system contains the receptors themselves that perceive the stimuli, such as eyes and ears and taste buds, plus a network of neurons that transmit and interpret the data. When you are touched, for example, neurons transmit the signal from the skin receptors to the brain, where other neurons evaluate the encounter. It is estimated that the total number of neuron connections in your brain far exceeds the number of stars in the Milky Way Galaxy. The degree of complexity in evaluating the most casual touch is staggering.

Our continued existence offers living proof that our senses have portrayed the world successfully enough to allow our survival. Have they told us the truth, the whole truth, and nothing but the truth? Have they shaded the truth, hidden the truth, or created vast realms of meaning from the flimsiest of clues? The story of You is endlessly fascinating.

Vision

If I had been placed on a committee to design our visual system, I would have kept it simple. Let light enter through the eyes, I would have said, and let the brain interpret the pattern of light that enters. However, our visual system was not constructed "the easy way." One of the surprises is that light itself, which seems to us to be the star of the show, is only involved in Act One. It instigates a cascade of nerve activity within us, and the whole remainder of the show is the firing of nerves.

Specifically, light enters the eyes, where it is absorbed and translated into neurological code. Nerves transmit the coded signal from the eyes to the brain, where a *virtual image* is constructed. It is this virtual image of the outside world constructed by our own brain that we perceive when we think we are viewing the world directly. Our body thereby takes a difficult problem - visualizing the outside world - creates an almost impossible solution, and accomplishes this prestidigitation so seamlessly that we don't realize a virtual image has been substituted for a real one. In fact, all our perceptions of the outside world are representations created by the firing patterns of nerves within our brain.

Let us consider how light, like the ghost of Hamlet's father, sets in motion a chain of events in which it only participates as an initiator. 93 million miles away, a little over eight minutes ago, thermonuclear processes within the Sun sent light streaming into the vacuum of space, crossing the orbits of Mercury and Venus before entering the atmosphere of Earth. Or, perhaps, the light traveled 8 feet from a nearby light bulb. A split second ago, the mixture of wavelengths that make up solar light (or its man-made counterpart) struck the grass, where part of the light was absorbed. A tiny fraction of the rest, reflected by the grass, entered the pupil of your eye and was focused by the lens onto the retina. The retina, a thin layer of tissue at the back of each eyeball, contains light receptor cells called rods and cones, and also many nerves.

When the sunlight reflected by the grass falls upon the retinal rods and cones and is absorbed there, its cosmic journey is ended. The retinal rod and cone light-absorption pattern is encoded into the activation of nerves from the eye to the brain. *Receiving this neurological input but no light, the brain constructs our entire experience of visual reality.*

An auditory analogy, suggested by my friend George Palmer, would be a phone conversation. [165] Let's say your Aunt Minnie is calling you from Cleveland. Although it sounds like Minnie's voice in the earpiece of your phone, you realize the actual sound of her voice could not be heard beyond the walls of her apartment. Rather, her telephone deconstructed her voice and translated it into a series of impulses that could be rapidly transmitted by electrical wires or radio waves to the phone in your bedroom, where the patterns of her voice are reconstituted by your telephone receiver into a facsimile that sounds like Minnie. With a moment's thought, you realize that the sounds you hear on the phone cannot really be Minnie's actual voice carrying all the way from Cleveland, but rather a reconstruction of that voice in the earpiece.

Of course, telephones are designed so that the sound you hear through the earpiece is "rigged" to affect your sensory system in the same way that Aunt Minnie's voice does. The facsimile, therefore, accurately represents her voice. In the real world, we do not know the true nature of external reality, and therefore can't know how accurately our senses portray it. Translating from our auditory analogy to our visual system, we live in a world we are not allowed to see directly, and survive on the basis of our ability to construct effective facsimiles.

Further we do not experience the grass - or anything else - by the color it "is," but by the wavelengths of light that it has reflected. Isaac Newton used a prism to demonstrate that sunlight, which appears clear to us, actually contains all the colors of the rainbow. The light that illuminates our planet is actually a concoction of all the rainbow's colors, which when mixed together appear clear and colorless to our vision.

"Green" grass and leaves absorb the wavelengths of sunlight that we call "red" and "blue" to run the process of photosynthesis that sustains their life. The rest - the wavelengths they reflect - are the wavelengths that strike our eye and which our brain perceives as green. *There is nothing about the grass itself that is intrinsically green.* One might say that green is the color the grass itself *is not*, representing the wavelengths it has discarded. *In fact, everything we see appears to us the color we ascribe to the wavelengths it has not absorbed, but rather reflected.*

Our visual perception of "reality" is obviously different in the dark of night than in the bright light of day, because a different set of retinal light receptors is activated. The rods are more numerous (120 million), more sensitive in low light conditions, more widespread throughout the retina, but provide only indistinct images in shades of black, white, and gray. Our "night vision" is rod vision. The cones number only 6 million, are mostly located in the central retinal region called the macula, require more light than rods do to be activated, but provide our crisp, sharp, daytime color vision (the cones are also activated by bright artificial light).

It is unlikely that the objects of the external world intrinsically exist in the colors by which we perceive them. Our brain paints its virtual images with color, which does not have to accurately represent extrinsic reality to be useful. It allows greater contrast in our viewing and therefore better identification of the borders of external objects, so we do not have to try to identify threat and opportunity in a sea of gray images. Even false colorization allows easy identification of red apples against a backdrop of green leaves, instead of gray against gray.

Each retinal rod and cone serves as a single pixel in the eventual creation of a visual image, and each has neurological connections to a specific set of neurons in the brain. Each pixel only has meaning in relationship to the other pixels, so all pattern discrimination must be done in the brain rather than the eye. Dr. Norden estimates that about one billion bits of information pass from the eye to the brain each second, and the brain must ignore almost all of them. It must preferentially scan the data for what is new or changing and therefore of potentially acute significance. [166]

Approximately 30 different areas of the brain are involved in processing the image, each specializing in analyzing specific features of the incoming signal. These brain regions fragment the image like a cubist painting, scanning for edges, for contrast, for familiar patterns such as faces, and - in particular - for motion. From such information, shape, location, and velocity of external objects can be deduced as the brain then fuses the fragmented components back into the single visual reconstruction of the outside world that we perceive. Dr. Norden states, "You don't see with your eye. You see with your brain." [167] *From the pattern of light falling on the retinal rods and cones, deconstructed, transmitted via electrochemical code by nerves to the brain, separately analyzed as fragmented pieces of data and then reconstructed, the brain generates virtual visual images, colorizes them, and presents them to our conscious awareness.* Think about the complexity involved in every step. Yet this is what happens each time you see something "with your own eyes."

Consider how rapidly visual images change, as if we are watching a smoothly flowing moving picture of the outside world rather than a slide show. All the electrochemical processes within the eye and brain must not only occur quickly, but also degrade and remodel almost instantaneously to continually allow the generation of new images. You are not forced to survive this moment based on the visual images generated several seconds ago, because the visual system continually transitions from "old" images of a moment ago to the current ones on display now. After all, an animal that processes sensory data slowly ends up on another animal's menu.

Clearly the model of external reality that our visual system creates must get a lot of things right. We can drive automobiles in traffic or play tennis, so our conceptualization of shapes, distances, and velocities must be accurate. We could not share highways with other cars if other drivers did not form similar spatial conceptions of external reality. Essentially all the animal kingdom that is exposed to sunlight uses it to create visual models of their environment, and even many plants array themselves based on the position of the sun. However, other animal species colorize their visual images with different cone chemistry and, of course, with different brains than we do, so it is probable that they view the same external world through a different color scheme.

Look at the grass outside your window again. Consider that your visual system is likely generating an extremely accurate model of the shape and location of the grass. It is colorizing the grass the shade we call green, a color most people find attractive. We are even imbued with a sense of beauty that is activated by such a "vision."

Now contemplate other features that come as standard equipment for your eyes. Tear ducts keep the membranes on the outer surface of the eye from drying out and provide a flood of tears to wash away irritants like dust. Eyebrows channel perspiration away from the eyes, and eyelashes reduce the risk of dust entering. The pupil constricts or dilates to regulate the amount of light entering the system, and thereby protects the retina. Your eye comes equipped with a lens that changes shape to focus light on the retina, whether the object of your vision is inches or miles away. Sets of muscles coordinate the eyes to quickly move in tandem and generate a single sharp three-dimensional image. Incredibly, preset regions of the brain exist to receive and instantly analyze data.

Yet when people comment on their eyes, it is usually in regards to their imperfections. Visual problems certainly increase with age and are discussed commonly; I do not recall anyone ever mentioning how amazing their eyes are. It is when they fall short of perfection that we notice our eyes and think of them as a problem rather than a blessing. When we use perfection as a standard of comparison, even our eyes seem to be a burden. We notice the flaw and miss the miracle.

A good form of meditation would be to look in a mirror at your own eyes, with your own eyes, and think about what you are accomplishing.

Sound

Since we have lived immersed in sound from the day of our birth, it seems like only a lunatic could question to what extent sound actually exists. Yet the familiar riddle about whether a tree that falls in the middle of a forest creates sound if there are no listeners hints at deeper questions. Is sound a real entity that exists in the outside world or the internal subjective experience of a listener? Does our sense of hearing detect sound or create it?

The sense of hearing is definitely a system that detects *vibrations*. Whether it actually detects sound, or whether sound even exists in the world outside ourselves, cannot be tested. Every sound you hear emanates from a source that is vibrating. The slam of a door, the rustle of leaves, the words of a friend are all audible because an initial vibrating source creates waves in an intervening medium such as air or water. These waves cause components within your ear to vibrate, activating the firing of nerves to the auditory centers of your brain. The brain then translates these nerve patterns into the subjective experience of sound. I again quote Dr. Norden: "Sound is a construction of your brain." [168]

The best human ears can detect a vibratory range from about 15 cycles per second to about 20,000 cycles per second, all of which we perceive as sound. Leaves that rustle in the wind are being blown about on their branches, strumming against each other, setting each other vibrating. Or - to be more mathematical - imagine a pianist pressing down on the key of Middle C, causing a hammer to strike a string and set it vibrating at just under 262 cycles per second. The acoustics of the piano provide a full, rich resonance, but unless there is a medium such as air to transmit the vibrations to the ear of a listener, there is only silence.

Each vibration of the piano string toward your ears pushes some air molecules together into a cluster and knocks that cluster of slightly higher pressure air toward your ear. As the string then vibrates back away from you, it creates a gap or partial vacuum of slightly thinner air. With each vibration toward you, the string knocks another high-pressure air cluster in your direction, followed by a gap of lower pressure as the string vibrates away from you. Since the string vibrates at 262 cycles per second, it has created and knocked outward each second a sequence of 262 clusters of high air pressure alternating with 262 gaps of lower pressure, and these alternating pressure waves move outward at the "speed of sound," about 1,000 feet per second in room temperature air. In reality, no individual molecules travel very far, or we would be struck by enormous winds with every sound. Instead, air molecules are like a standing row of dominoes; the first domino topples the second, which topples the third, and so on, without any domino moving very far. Air molecules transmitting the energy from the vibrating piano string are pushed into nearby air molecules, which in turn are pushed into the next air molecules, which are pushed into the next, in the path from the source toward the ear of the listener. The pressure variation between the regions of high pressure and those of low pressure associated with a sound wave differ from each other by about *one part in 10 million*, and from this infinitesimal variance, we comprehend spoken language and listen to symphonies and polkas.

As the waves of minute alternations in air pressure are about to reach your ear, let us pause and ask if sound exists "out there" in the world if there is no listener. In fact, the process of sound highlights the dramatic difference between the state of external reality and our perception of that reality. Out in the world, there are vibrating sources such as our piano string, and waves of alternating high and low pressure that the sources generate. Does this passage of pressure waves through the air, in the absence of listeners, qualify as sound? Dr. Norden firmly states her opinion: "The answer is no, sound is what our brain creates from vibrations that affect receptors, which then transmit this information to the brain." [169] Sound is a subjective experience that requires a vibrating source, a conducting medium, and the auditory apparatus of a listener. Take away any one of these - such as the listener - and sound does not exist.

But let us now follow those alternating air pressure waves generated by the vibrating piano string as they strike the ear of the listener. The eardrum, a membrane between the outer and middle ear, is knocked inward 262 times a second by the power of the clusters of compressed air, while alternately springing back outward 262 times a second when the lessened air pressure of the "gaps" allows it to do so. The eardrum has been set into vibration at the same frequency as the source, the piano string. Three tiny bones in the middle ear portray the role of additional dominoes to carry the wave forward at that same frequency. The first of these bones, the malleus, is stuck to the back of the eardrum. The malleus, with each vibration of the eardrum, is knocked into the second bone, the incus, which is knocked into the third bone, the stapes (the tiniest bone in the human body). These are special dominoes that automatically reset themselves into their original position after each wave, allowing them to receive and transmit hundreds or thousands of waves per second.

The stapes is driven inward with each vibration, 262 times a second in our example, into the membrane lining the fluid-filled inner ear, where sits the Organ of Corti. To this point, the air molecules, eardrum, and the three bones of the middle ear have served as a mechanism for transmitting to the inner ear the vibratory frequency of the source. One could consider to what extent sound exists even at this stage, as a piano string vibrates and generates pressure waves that emanate outward to set into vibration components within the ear of a listener.

The Organ of Corti is one of the most important organs within the human body that the average person has never heard of. While livers and pancreases snatch all the headlines, the Organ of Corti begins the metamorphosis of this chain of vibrations into the subjective experience of sound. Along the length of the Organ of Corti, a row of 12,000 to 20,000 "hair cells" extends out from a basilar membrane.

The hair cells and basilar membrane serve as a sort of keyboard, where each region has a different frequency of incoming vibrations to which it optimally resonates. Nerves associated with the hair cells are then triggered to fire when their hair cells have been activated by the incoming vibrations, and they transmit to the brain the news that incoming vibrations of a particular frequency have been detected. In our example, hair cells that optimally vibrate at 262 cycles per second are set into their maximal vibration by the piano's Middle C, and their adjacent nerve notifies the brain, conveying the coded message, "Incoming vibrations at 262 cycles per second received!" From this information, *the brain is thought to construct the subjective experience we call sound.*

This is known as the "place principle" of sound pitch, in which gradations in stiffness at a particular place in the Organ of Corti determines which hair cells will be turned on as a consequence of the specific vibratory rate of the source. Increased sound volume is probably the result of more forceful vibrations, which activate more hair cells and vibrate them faster and more vigorously, stimulating more nerve activation to the brain.

Again, alchemy is at work. It is the brain that translates vibrations emanating from the outside world into our subjective experience of sound. Our brains devote a disproportionately large amount of their auditory capacity to the wavelengths of the human voice range. Thus the auditory system, initially a means of detecting vibrations, becomes the gateway to language, which in turn launched our species out of caves and into skyscrapers. While the brains of most animal species perform the trick of converting vibrations into the perceptual experience of sound, the human brain is undoubtedly special. Near the "primary auditory cortex," the part of the brain's temporal lobes that receives neurological input from the ear, the human brain features specialized language centers that have developed the improbable skill of turning vibratory input into linguistic meaning.

In every conversation, a speaker's vocal cord vibrations create pressure waves of air, and then these waves are shaped with movements of the jaw, mouth, and lips to encode meaning. The vibrations transmit the signal through waves of air molecules to eventually vibrate hair cells in the listener's Organ of Corti, which turns incoming vibrations into the firing of nerves headed to the language centers of the listener's brain. There the signal is decoded and meaning extracted; other regions of the brain pitch in to formulate a reply. Back and forth, ideas are exchanged via pressure waves shaped by the mouth of the speaker, carried by air molecules, encoded and decoded by language centers within the brain.

We are the agents through which this remarkable process happens all the time. Equally remarkable is our lack of insight into how amazing this capability is. We pay attention to the content of speech but don't realize that the mechanism seems like science fiction. The gift comes to us so easily that we do not recognize it as a gift.

Although vision gives a more accurate picture of our immediate surroundings than we gain through our auditory sense, language allows the possibility of sharing and storing information. Spoken language was the tool that powered the rise of culture, allowing subsequent generations to build upon the foundation of previously gained knowledge. If anyone learns a truth or technological skill, language allows everyone in the culture to share that step forward. Human culture was far advanced before the widespread use of written language. Certainly interpersonal relationships revolve almost entirely around spoken language, a natural gift shared by almost everyone the world over.

So, what happens when that oft-contemplated tree falls in the middle of the forest and no one is there to hear? Is there sound? One answer is that any real forest has plenty of non-human listeners such as birds and squirrels, who surely can construct the subjective experience of sound out of the vibrations emanating from the falling tree. If we remove all conscious life from the no-longer-real forest, do the vibrations of the fallen tree and the resultant outward waves of air compressions separated by lower pressure gaps constitute the real existence of sound in the absence of listeners?

When most people conceptualize the world, they instinctively presume sound is a "thing-in-itself" that surely exists in the outside world or we would not be able to hear it. Such people would presume a falling tree would generate sound that would be a real, if temporary, feature of the forest, and would most certainly exist whether a listener was present or not. A different conception arises if sound is considered an *interaction* between component parts, which only exists if all the components are present. Understood in this way, sound requires a vibrating source (a falling tree qualifies), a transmitting medium such as air to conduct the vibrations, a vibration receiver such as an ear (absent from this hypothetical forest), and a brain perceiver (also absent). Only if all its components are present can sound exist, so the absence of a listener prevents the existence of sound, no matter how many trees fall. The forest would then have falling trees creating air pressure waves, but no mechanism for converting those vibrations into the subjective experience of sound. Although the ultimate truth of either proposition cannot be tested, the most likely scenario is considered to be the latter one, in which sound does not exist unless all its components are present, including a listener.

Sound thereby likely joins color as features that seem to be part of the outside world, but instead are most likely add-ons that sentient beings create and apply to their perceptions. Just as we paint our visual experiences with color, we likewise turn the world's vibrations into sound. Most animals have some mechanism for performing this transformation, at varying degrees of proficiency. The ability of our species to further translate vibrations into complex language represents a double leap, a stunning feat of creativity. The outside world provides vibrations; we turn those vibrations into sound and sound into language, and in doing so, take a giant stride toward becoming human.

Let us take an easier question. What happens if we have a source of vibrations and a potential listener, but no medium to transmit the vibrations? For example, imagine there was a vacuum separating you from the pianist. The vibrations created by the pianist could not cross the vacuum to reach your ear. Your eardrum would not be deflected and the rest of your hearing mechanism would not be activated. The sonata would seem to be totally silent to you. Move the world's loudest bell into the vacuum of outer space and ring it as forcefully as you can, and the result will be silence when there is no medium to transmit the bell's vibration to the ear of a potential listener.

Yet we do not live in a vacuum or in isolation. Every moment, our sense of hearing links us to a world that is filled with vibrations. We channel and create some of these vibrations through language and music. At the source of every sound we hear, something is vibrating, ultimately causing our own auditory system to vibrate in synchrony, at the same frequency. It is as if our auditory system is itself a musical instrument played by the vibrations of the world. Considered in this way, the outside world becomes the "musician" that creates vibrations, and we become the instrument that turns those vibrations into sound. Listen again to the world, thoughtfully, appreciatively.

Smell

Any celebration of our alleged superiority as a species must quickly skim over the sense of smell, at which we are decidedly second tier. Many animals in nature rely heavily on a marvelous sense of smell, a sense that is useful but not critical to human survival. As with most of our sensory experiences, an unpleasant olfactory experience motivates us to avoid the source, be it rotten food or a skunk. Communicating via airborne chemicals or identifying the objects of the outside world by the substances they release is not a skill at which we excel.

Molecules commonly break away from their source and make their way into the environment, providing clues to any olfactory Sherlock Holmes who can deduce their origin. Within the cells inside our noses are proteins, often similar but not identical, that serve as a chemistry lab. Human noses have hundreds of proteins that can react (or not) with any incoming molecule, called an odorant, that floats in on the air. Each protein is a long chain of amino acids that folds into a complex three-dimensional shape, generating within the protein multiple different local regions and pockets called domains. To activate a protein nasal receptor, an incoming odorant must have the right shape, size, solubility and electrical charge to fit like a puzzle piece into a domain in the protein. If the particle does not fit into any of the proteins, it is odorless. If it does fit, the odorant acts as a key fitting into the protein's lock, causing the protein to change shape and send a coded report of its activation via a nerve to the brain. The brain adds up all the proteins voting "Yes," and the result of this tabulation is the subjective experience of a particular odor. Each odor represents a specific coalition of proteins activated by that odorant.

In spite of all that, in olfactory skill, we are much less talented than our dog. The lining of a dog's nostril contains about 100 scent-sensitive nerves for every one of ours per cubic centimeter, plus a greater variety of scent-detecting protein receptors. Dogs in general can detect concentrations of odorants over 100,000 times fainter than our own noses can detect, and certain breeds such as bloodhounds can do even better. [170]

Nothing in the world has an objective odor. Each odor is a subjective experience of a perceiver detecting molecules or chemical compounds released by a source. My dog, with a more sensitive olfactory system than me, perceives the same odorant differently than I do. For example, a rose releases molecules into the air. The olfactory experience of those molecules is different for a bee, for my dog, and for me.

Nature features many different odor detection systems. Bears likely surpass even bloodhounds at this talent. Fish appear to have a good sense of smell, detecting odorants in water. Insects detect odorants through their antennae, from which nerves carry data to their brain. Moths may be the long-distance champions; males' antennae can pick up molecules secreted by females three miles away. The fragrances of plants are lures to attract pollinating insects.

Science journalist Tim Friend in *Animal Talk* defines a pheromone as "any substance secreted by an organism outside its body that causes a specific reaction in another organism of the same species …" Friend points out, "The most important signal for many species of insects and mammals is the pheromone …" which typically relies on the olfactory system for detection. [171] In colonies of bees and ants, the queen releases pheromones that dictate sexual mating and work schedules throughout the colony. Female cats "in heat" release chemicals that notify male cats all over the neighborhood of their sexual availability.

Friend reports that adult female elephants are strongly attracted to the smelliest males. Amorous male elephants in turn monitor the odor of urine from females, seeking to detect a chemical that signals sexual readiness in the female and optimizes the male's likelihood of getting a date with her. Many interactions in nature occur through such chemical conversations to which we are oblivious.

It is controversial to what extent our own species responds to odors of the other sex. Friend reports on studies that indicate women might be attracted to a musky androgen-induced odor in men. [172] The attraction females feel toward the smelliest males may provide an effective strategy for elephants, but humans go to great lengths to erase natural odors or cover them with artificial ones. The perfume, cologne, toothpaste, and deodorant industries (among others) demonstrate the extent to which humans wish to eradicate body odors that may represent a certain primal animal quality we seek to leave behind.

In any event, our blend of talents and sensibilities has reduced our reliance on the sense of smell. However, it certainly does work in tandem with our other specialized chemical detection kit, our sense of taste, in screening the outside world for our next meal.

Taste

Our bodies are composed of atoms, and our only sources of those atoms are the air we breathe and the food we eat. Although we can have a long-term impact on the pollutants we put into the air that we will breathe in the future, for today we have no choice but to breathe the atmosphere as it currently is. In regards to food, we have many choices. We must obtain every element that is critical to sustaining our life and avoid the toxins that would make us ill or even kill us. Particularly for animals living in nature, this would seem to require a brilliant knowledge of chemistry and biology. Yet via genetically encoded instincts and the sense of taste, we live and thrive.

Remarkably, the products of Earth that improve survival when ingested usually do taste good. As mentioned previously, if eating carrots improves a rabbit's survival, rabbits that find carrots tasty and eat more of them will be more successful at living and reproducing. Rabbits that crave the taste of toxic metals will not survive to reproduce. The sense of taste over time incorporates the genetic endowment of the survivors and guides their descendants regarding what to ingest to build their bodies and what to avoid.

Our caveman ancestors did not have supermarkets to guarantee the safety and quality of their food, nor did animals in the forest. They, like us, were equipped with the means to test food via their sense of taste. Our personal test lab for screening food before swallowing it comes in the form of taste buds located primarily on the tongue and soft palate, each consisting of about 50-100 taste cells. It was once thought that different areas of the tongue specialized in detecting specific flavors, but it is now believed that taste buds in all parts of the tongue can detect each of the categories of flavor. The four major qualities of taste are sweet, sour, bitter, and salty, to which a fifth category called umami has been added by Japanese researchers. Umami is translated as "meaty" or "savory," and represents the presence of glutamate, which is found in meats and fish and the flavor enhancer monosodium glutamate.

When food enters the mouth, its chemicals - called "tastants" - must be dissolved in saliva to interact with the taste cells. The rest of the process evokes similarities to the mechanism of the sense of smell. Taste cells contain proteins curled into three-dimensional shapes. Dissolved tastants react with domains of specific protein receptors into which they fit "like a key in a lock," according to neuroscientist David V. Smith and molecular biologist Robert F. Margolskee. [173] This is reminiscent of the mechanism by which odorants fit into nasal receptors to mediate the sense of smell. When turned on by a tastant with the appropriate shape and electrical charge, the receptor proteins set in motion the firing of nerves at the base of each activated taste bud to relay the message to the brain. Again, the brain tabulates all the "Affirmative" votes from activated taste cells, and the sum is the subjective perception of a particular flavor. Peanut butter sandwiches reliably taste like peanut butter sandwiches because they activate the same combination of receptors each time.

The flavors we perceive would then primarily represent combinations of sweet, sour, bitter, salty, and if glutamate is present, umami. Each activated taste cell would report on specific qualities of the tastant, such as its saltiness, via neurological messages to the brain, where input from these separate channels is

196

integrated into the overall perception of taste. This information would be further merged with sensory data about a food's smell, texture, temperature, and visual appearance in our conscious experience of a meal, which we further judge to be pleasant (with hopes of repeating the experience) or distasteful (warning - avoid in the future!).

Is there a reason why our oral taste kit assesses a potential meal in terms of the qualities of sweet, sour, bitter, and salty? Why not peppery, cheesy, or buttery? Might there be some special survival value in the combination we utilize?

The serum within our blood vessels is a saltwater solution, so maintenance of adequate salt intake is a critical life-preserving function. It cannot be a coincidence that most people find moderately salted food pleasurable. Rather famously, soldiers of the Roman Empire were paid in salt, from which our word "salary" derives.

On the other hand, acids activate the "sour" receptors in our mouth. To survive, we must keep the acidity of our blood in a very narrow range. We are prevented from accidentally ingesting too much acid into our system by the unpleasant sour taste it induces. Sweets tend to be high-calorie foods whose pleasurable taste creates motivation for further consumption, useful to marginally nourished individuals such as our prehistoric ancestors whose genes we have inherited. The ability to readily store excess calories as fat allowed our ancestors to survive famines, though we today are not so grateful for that ability. Numerous chemical compounds activate our "bitter" receptors; obviously this does not add to our dining pleasure, but warns us to avoid potentially toxic substances. Thus our chemical taste kit motivates us toward adequate salt and calorie intake and reduced acid ingestion, while screening out various potential toxins.

Taste is a uniquely personalized interaction between each animal and the food it consumes in order to live. All animals appear to be geniuses in biochemistry by following the dictates of their sense of taste. It rewards rabbits for eating carrots, whales for eating plankton, and dogs for chewing bones, as they build and maintain their bodies.

Our bodies also contain the wisdom of internal sensors that monitor our metabolic state and fluid balance, then influence our behavior. In the hypothalamus within the brain, the concentrations of chemicals such as salt in the blood are monitored. The blood vessels also send input to the brain about the volume of fluid they contain. If the fluid volume drops low or the salt concentration starts to rise, these detectors trigger the sensation of thirst and send us to the water fountain.

We are all aware of sensors that inform us through the sensation of hunger when we require more nutrients and calories. An empty stomach results in messages to the brain that mealtime - or at least snack time - is due. One such chemical messenger is called ghrelin, released by an empty stomach. An overfilled stomach suppresses brain hunger centers. Receptors sensitive to the levels of glucose, fats, or other metabolites also can drive or suppress appetite. Fat cells produce a chemical called leptin, which may curtail hunger. Various chemical stimulants and suppressants of appetite are the subject of active research.

Consider how you have assembled your body and continue to do so, incorporating all the necessary elements, avoiding dangerous toxins. Think about the entire animal kingdom that has done the same. What amazing internal wisdom you possess in maintaining your body! As you eat a meal, become aware of this food that is about to become You; be conscious of the sense of taste that has helped you choose which elements to incorporate into your future self. While your food selection was probably consciously driven by taste, a larger and deeper wisdom used that sense of taste in building your living, thinking body from the elements of the Earth.

The World Within

We learn a great deal about the outside world through our senses, but that is only part of the equation. Since all our sensory experiences are *interactions* between the outside world and us, we gain through each such interaction great insight into our own nature. Vision not only informs us about shapes and velocities "out there;" it also lets us realize that we have internal systems skilled at assessing the outside world via reflected sunlight. When we hear others speak, we certainly learn about the speaker and the topic she is discussing, but we can also recognize that we are experts at translating vocal cord vibrations into sound and meaningful symbolic language. As we walk outside on a winter's day, we appreciate that the skin that serves as our body's border is an intricate combination of sensors working in tandem with dedicated brain centers to monitor the environment in defense of our safety (perhaps a warmer sweater would be a good idea). We not only find a spaghetti dinner delicious, but may also realize that our sense of taste has run chemical tests on the spaghetti and found it to be an acceptable building block that we can safely ingest.

Nothing could be more routine, or more profound, than to observe the world with our senses. As you see, hear, feel, smell, and touch, think about the complex systems you have in place to be co-creator of those interactions, with the intellectual power to weave them into an understanding of the world and of your self. What remarkable internal wisdom you possess to know what you know and skillfully interpret your interplay with the universe. The fact that you accomplish all these feats so easily does not detract from the skill set you embody.

Open your senses. Observe outward. Observe inward. Repeat.

Conversation

Male humpback whales are famous for their complex songs, which contain multiple themes, last perhaps 30 minutes, and are detectable by sonar from several hundred miles away. All the males in a particular part of the ocean will sing the same song, with some individual variation and a tendency for modification over time. No one really knows what the singer is trying to express. Perhaps he is romancing a female or notifying other males of his location; perhaps he is just in the mood for a song.

199

Despite their vocal gifts, male humpbacks tend to be solitary creatures. They mate from time to time, perhaps transiently join loose social groups that might stay together for a few hours or days, but mostly travel the oceans alone. It is guessed that they may live 60 years or so on average, and much longer for some individuals, plenty of time for contemplation. What mental or emotional life might a whale experience as he spends so many years in pathless oceans by himself?

It is far from our human experience, for we were born to communicate. Most human infants are quick to develop relationships and have a natural gift for language skills that they eagerly embrace. We find richness in sharing our lives with others, and live immersed in the flow of words. Whether language is being used to convey deep feelings or insights, or merely to fill a few otherwise awkward empty minutes, the words flow relatively easily and naturally from our lips. Yet every aspect of a conversation, when thoughtfully considered, seems almost impossible.

Let us consider again the mechanism. Perhaps our conversation begins with my intent to speak to you. What is the nature of the "I" who wishes to speak? Is this "I" a focal region within my brain, or something much more nebulous and diffuse? Next comes the development of an idea, by an unknown mechanism, and my wish to share this idea. Parts of my brain activate, specifically those that have developed the special skill of encoding thoughts in symbols we call words. The sounds I will utter will not have any natural relationship to their meaning, but rather possess symbolic significance that has been defined by my culture. Still far beyond our understanding of process, I activate my vocal apparatus. Inanimate thought has bridged the chasm between intangible and tangible, and my respirations begin to coordinate with the vibrations of my vocal cords. I clearly am controlling at a certain level the process of vocalization, but I have no understanding of how I am generating meaningful sounds.

My vocal cords vibrate perhaps 100 times per second when I speak, though I don't consciously set that rate. I exhale as my cords vibrate, and use my mouth, tongue, lips, and teeth to give form to the waves of air pressure emitted from the back of my throat into the air outside my body. The air molecules, drifting aimlessly before I speak, become organized into pressure waves journeying at 100 vibrations per second, transmitting the waves from my vocal cords toward your ears. Through the air these waves travel, organizing the air molecules into a series of 100 cycle-per-second vibrations, until they strike your eardrum and set it vibrating at that same rate of 100 times per second. By mechanisms we have discussed, eventually the hair cells in your inner ear that maximally vibrate at 100 cycles per second will be activated, and fire off encoded nerve messages to your brain, reporting incoming vibrations at 100 cycles per second. The intensity of the vibrations determines how forcefully your eardrum is struck, which is translated into the volume of the sound that you will experience.

Your brain doesn't hear my words directly, but rather receives via nerves from your ears information about pitch, volume, and the verbal symbols I have somehow expressed as vibrations. Within your brain, the vibrations are converted into the subjective experience of sound, and the wave pattern is converted into meaning. Nerves fire. The intangible thought that began in my mind somehow activated nerves within me to trigger a sequence of physical vibrations - my vocal cords, air, your eardrum - to be translated back into nerve activation within your brain and decoded there back into intangible thought. How are we capable of such an operation?

You respond by mentally generating a reply, converting it into nerve activation that is translated into your own vocal cord vibration, and through a sequence of vibrations you send your message back to strike my eardrum and ultimately activate the set of nerves through which I comprehend your reply. Even if our words might be casual rather than profound, the process is impossibly complex. From intangible thought to sequenced nerve activations, through a series of vibrations, back into nerve activation, and ultimately to the decoding of vibrations. So goes the simplest conversation, back and forth, crossing the border of the incomprehensible multiple times in the most routine of interactions.

We do not perceive the miracle of our conversations because our attention is focused on the meaning. Yet most of us cannot help but be social creatures when such communication skills are intrinsic to our natures. Think how much the ability to converse has meant to you, and the ease with which this skill has allowed you to form meaningful relationships.

We understand that someone said "Hello" to us; we understand the content of their words. The sounds float to us on the surface of an ocean of mysterious processes. By skimming the words off the surface, we have gleaned a little information.

What does the ability to casually converse tell you about yourself? What has this skill meant to you in terms of enriching your life? Without this gift, our lives might parallel the humpback whale's, making his way through life alone.

Biography

Perhaps you might compose your biography something like this: begin with the date and place of birth, mention early family life and education, and proceed to career. List special honors and particular achievements, while including current circumstances. Of course, such an event-based biography omits almost everything that you ever did. It skips all the meals, the movies, the picnics, and reduces your story to a verbal caricature. None of the miracles that composed your life are mentioned. How do you think about your own life?

An abbreviated rough draft of a more accurate biography might follow this outline. Your father contributed a sperm, and your mother, an egg. Those microscopic cells merged into one DNA-containing cell, and that cell was you. Through trillions of cell divisions, you grew and developed over 200 types of specialized integrated cells interwoven into multiple organ systems. Each cell and organ activated the proper genes to dutifully perform its tasks.

Your first nine months were spent within the womb of your mother, one body within another; her nutrition was your nutrition. Then, on the day of your birth, you for the first time inhaled the atmosphere of the planet. You began shifting from getting all your nourishment from your mother to eating food provided by the dirt, air, and oceans. You drank water carried to Earth as ice on comets, and breathed oxygen created in the terminal explosions of extinct stars.

Within months you were communicating meaningfully, initially non-verbally. Then you began encoding thoughts into symbolic language as spoken words transmissible through air, enabling you to form relationships over the course of a lifetime. With a proud parent holding a camera, you fought off the pull of gravity and rose upright on wobbly legs. Gaining balance, you took coordinated steps, remaining vertical for two steps, four steps, a million steps. You smiled, and people smiled back at you. You reached out a hand and grasped a toy, a lollipop, another hand.

As different networks of cells within your body fired in synchrony, you experienced love for your family, forged friendships, and felt the surge of emotions. Brain neurons further linked into networks in the process we call learning. All this just seemed natural. Off to school you went, reading and writing with symbolic notation, equipped with brain language centers that no other species in the history of the world could match. At every meal, you incorporated atoms and energy into your own growing body, as age-appropriate genes turned on and off in all your cells in your passage through the years. Hundreds, thousands of chemical reactions transpired within your cells, adjusting as internally controlled metabolic pathways altered to meet your needs.

You acquired a unique set of skills, passions, and relationships that reflect the gifts and talents afforded by a physical body. With ease you extracted nutrients and oxygen from the outside world, and generated thoughts.

In your voyage of discovery, you continue to explore a life-sustaining planet as you share your journey with others whose hearts beat in bodies of their own. Without conscious effort, your body has created lungs, bones, a heart, thousands of miles of blood vessels, a liver and kidneys. You didn't stop with the major structures, but went on to make teeth of different shapes, eyelashes, hormones, toenails, taste buds, and sensitive fingertips. This very day and moment are yours.

You have the power to define what is important in your life. You certainly possess the intelligence to recognize how unique you are in the entire universe. Don't settle for a smaller story of your life. Your biography is astounding, and it is still a work-in-progress. Recognize in your simplest act the miracle of what you are accomplishing. *You are stardust dancing.*

CONCLUSION AND BEGINNING

We shall not cease from exploration
And at the end of all our exploring
Will be to arrive where we started
And know the place for the first time.

T. S. Eliot
"Four Quartets"

And while stars and waves have something to say
It's through my mouth they'll say it

Vicente Huidobro
"Something to Say"

The one life, the one consciousness,
takes on the form of a man or woman,
a blade of grass, a dog,
a planet, a sun, a galaxy....
This is the play of forms,
the dance of life.

Eckhart Tolle
Guardians of Being

Bunched Together

Joel R. Primack and Nancy Ellen Abrams state, "It's only because humans are all bunched together on one planet that we fail to see how extraordinary we are." [174] A similar point can be made about the days of our lives, which all come bunched together, so we do not recognize them as remarkable. If we were locked in an isolation chamber almost all the time and only released one day out of every 10 to be free in the world, we would appreciate what an amazing place the world is on that 10th day. If the world were barren and lifeless except for our solitary self 9 days out of 10, and filled with people and birds and dogs and flowers on the 10th day, we would recognize that a planet bursting with life is a rare gift.

If we could not communicate with each other except one day out of 10, we would prize that opportunity and speak from our hearts. If there were no music except on infrequent holidays, we would treasure those days. If the sun shone one day a year, we would feast our eyes while we could, before another year of darkness ensued. If we could only experience friendship and love once in a blue moon, how we would long for those moments. If we could only see or hear or taste one day a month, those sensory experiences would feel like superpowers.

Yet our days, filled with all those blessings and more, come bunched together. We do not have an isolation chamber to block us from access to the wonders of the world, so one day seems much like another, so very ordinary. We become blind to gifts that are in plain sight, because they are always there. Hence it would require an act of imagination to picture a world without these blessings, a world without sunshine or friendship or life. Such an act would allow us to appreciate that our world actually contains all these things, and we are free every day to experience them. They are all bunched together, accessible here and now, today and tomorrow. You have been given a living body to experience this amazing place, and the freedom to do it now. You only have to be yourself and perceive the world as it is.

Sometimes I sit in the back yard and close my eyes, just for the joy of opening them again.

Connections

We can view anything in the world, not just as an isolated entity, but also through its relationships. From this viewpoint, the parts of the universe that we name as separate can equally be viewed as links in a giant network.

What is the extent of a tree? Its physical boundaries appear evident; above ground it stands before you, while its roots, though hidden, would certainly seem to be of finite extent. However, the tree can be viewed as a way that Earth, air, Sun, and rain interact. The tree "breathes" carbon dioxide from the air while drawing vital elements through its roots from the Earth. Rain contributes water that dissolves and circulates molecules extracted from soil and air, while the sun's heat and light provide life-giving energy. The tree is what it is because Sun, Earth, air, and water are what they are. The Sun is what it is because galaxies are what they are, manifestations of a universe. The water that enters the roots is there because oceans, winds, clouds, and gravity are what they are, after ancient comets brought to Earth frozen water from the far reaches of the solar system and beyond.

Viewed in this way, a tree is a connection not only between Earth, Sun, air, and rain, but also between gravity, comets, and galaxies, an expression of processes that extend to the end of the universe. Rain connects ocean and Earth, Earth connects Sun and life, life connects Earth and air and Sun, and all are manifest in the tree.

We ourselves are equally interwoven in this network of mystery and miracle. In the words of David Suzuki, "It is impossible to draw lines that delineate separate categories of air, water, soil and life. You and I don't end at our fingertips or skin - we are connected through air, water and soil; we are animated by the same energy from the same source...." [175]

Fritjof Capra describes the "bootstrap hypothesis" of physicist Geoffrey Chew: "In the new world-view, the universe is seen as a dynamic web of interrelated events. None of the properties of any part of this web is fundamental; they all follow from the properties of the other parts, and the overall consistency of their mutual interrelations determines the structure of the entire web." [176]

That is, the nature of each part of the universe is dependent upon the properties of the rest of the universe. We are what we are because the rest of the universe is what it is, and the rest of the universe expresses itself in us, in the tree, in sun and rain. We are a link through which the entire cosmos connects, and are likewise a manifestation of sun, comets, and galaxies. The single interconnected web that includes us extends throughout space to the ends of the universe, a mesh of interwoven parts that continually change form. Through us, the ancient past makes its way toward the unforeseeable future. Each form not only is what it is, but connects everything else, manifests everything else. Our life and intelligence are the expression of an entire universe, making us cosmic in our extent and nature.

We are mortal, imperfect. Yet, as biochemist Robert S. deRopp writes, "In developed man the cosmic process becomes conscious of itself." [177] You, the perceiver and the perceived, can call it what you like, as long as you do not try to shrink the Infinite to small language and pretend it can be contained in words. You cannot even capture your own true nature in words. (Try it - any words you choose to describe yourself will sound like a trite cliché.) It does not seem possible that we could exist, but in our world, nothing is commoner than the seemingly impossible.

Feel the Infinite manifest itself in you. It is through you that the universe takes conscious form. The molecules that compose your body have passed through stars, rock, sky, interstellar space, and ocean in their long journey to this moment. The universe experiences life through you, breathes through you, sees through you, ponders Eternity through you. It is through you that the universe gains the consciousness to perceive, but never fully understand, its own deep mystery. More amazing than a million lifeless galaxies is the living consciousness that is you.

We touch the miraculous when we realize our own true identity.

What Next?

You have been a long time in the making. First there was a universe that gave rise to our galaxy, from which Earth condensed. From the elements of Earth, you were formed. It has taken the entire history of the universe to produce you and develop your talents, to bring you to life and present you with this moment. Use the opportunity. Be what you are, and recognize what you are, the product of billions of years of development, the expression of an entire universe.

Every moment since the dawn of the universe has laid the groundwork for you, your next thought, your next word. What will it be?

BIBLIOGRAPHY

Abbey, Edward. *Desert Solitaire*. New York: Ballantine, 1968.

The American Heritage Dictionary of the English Language. 4th Ed. Boston: Houghton Mifflin, 2006.

Attenborough, David. *Life on Earth*. Boston: Little, Brown, 1979.

---. *The Private Life of Plants*. Princeton: Princeton University Press, 1995.

Barrow, John D. *The Artful Universe Expanded*. Oxford, UK: Oxford University Press, 2005.

Bennett, Jeffrey, Seth Shostak, & Bruce Jakosky. *Life in the Universe*. San Francisco: Addison Wesley, 2003.

Bjornerud, Marcia. *Reading the Rocks*. Cambridge, Massachusetts: Westview, 2005.

Borges, Jorge Luis. "Poem of the Fourth Element." *Selected Poems*. Ed. A. Coleman. New York: Penguin, 1999.

Calvino, Italo. *Cosmicomics*. San Diego: Harcourt Brace Jovanovich, 1965.

Cameron, Julia. *The Artist's Way*. New York: Penguin Putnam, 1992.

Capra, Fritjof. *The Tao of Physics*. New York: Bantam, 1975.

Carroll, Sean B. *Endless Forms Most Beautiful*. New York: W.W. Norton, 2005.

---. "Regulating Evolution." *Scientific American*, May 2008: 60-67.

Cox, Brian & Andrew Cohen. *Wonders of the Universe*. New York: HarperCollins, 2011.

Dass, Ram. *Still Here*. New York: Penguin Putnam, 2000.

DeLillo, Don. *White Noise*. New York: Penguin, 1985.

de Montaigne, Michel, 1500s.

deRopp, Robert S. *The Warrior's Way*. New York: Dell, 1979.

Diener, Ed and Robert Biswas-Diener. *Happiness*. Malden, Massachusetts: Blackwell, 2008.

Dillard, Annie. *Pilgrim at Tinker Creek*. Toronto: Bantam, 1974.

Doidge, Norman, M.D. *The Brain That Changes Itself*. New York: Penguin, 2007.

Eiseley, Loren. *The Immense Journey*. New York: Vintage, 1953.

Foster, Russell G. and Leon Kreitzman. *Rhythms of Life*. New Haven: Yale University Press, 2004.

Friend, Tim. *Animal Talk*. New York: Free Press, 2004.

Gingras, Pierre. *The Secret Lives of Birds*. Willowdale, Ontario, Canada: Firefly, 1997.

Goodenough, Ursula. *The Sacred Depths of Nature*. Oxford, UK: Oxford University Press, 1998.

Hawking, Stephen. *A Brief History of Time*. New York: Bantam, 1988.

Heat-Moon, William Least. *Blue Highways*. Boston: Houghton Mifflin, 1982.

---. *Prairy Erth*. Boston: Houghton Mifflin, 1991.

Helmenstine, Anne Marie.
<http://chemistry.about.com/b/2011/02/06/how-much-are-the-elements-in-your-body-worth.htm>, 6 Feb. 2011.

Johnson, Steven. *Mind Wide Open*. New York: Scribner, 2004.

Kornfield, Jack. *Buddha's Little Instruction Book*. New York: Bantam, 1994.

Langer, Jiri. *Nine Gates to the Chassidic Mysteries*. New York: Behrman House, 1976.

Layard, Richard. *Happiness*. New York: Penguin, 2005.

Leary, Timothy. Informal talk at Rice University, Houston, Texas. ~ 1967.

Lewin, Roger. *Complexity*. Chicago: University of Chicago Press, 1999.

Logan, William Bryant. *Dirt*. New York: W.W. Norton, 1995.

Lutyens, Mary. *Krishamurti: The Years of Fulfilment*. New York: Farrar, Straus, Giroux, 1983.

Marent, Thomas. *Butterfly*. London: DK Publishing, 2008.

Mlodinow, Leonard. *The Drunkard's Walk*. New York: Pantheon, 2008.

Murchie, Guy. *The Seven Mysteries of Life*. Boston: Houghton Mifflin, 1981.

Norden, Jeanette, Ph.D. *Understanding the Brain* - DVD and Course Guidebook. Chantilly, Virginia: The Teaching Co., 2007.

Oliver, Mary. "Wild Geese," *New and Selected Poems, Volume One*. Boston: Beacon, 1992.

Osho. *The Spiritual Path.* Lewes, UK: Ivy Press, 2007.

Palmer, George. Informal conversation, Dallas, Texas, 2012.

Pirsig, Robert. *Zen and the Art of Motorcycle Maintenance.* New York: Bantam, 1974.

Pollard, Katherine S. "What Makes Us Human?" *Scientific American,* May 2009: 44-49.

Primack, Joel R., and Nancy Ellen Abrams. *The View From the Center of the Universe.* New York: Riverhead, 2006.

Ricklefs, Robert. *The Economy of Nature,* 4th Ed. New York: W.H. Freeman, 1994.

Ridley, Matt. *Genome.* New York: Perennial, 1999.

Schappert, Phil. *A World for Butterflies.* Buffalo, New York: Firefly, 2000.

Smith, David V., and Robert F. Margolskee. "Making Sense of Taste." *Scientific American,* 18 Mar. 2001.

Snyder, Gary. *A Place in Space.* Washington, DC: Counterpoint, 1995.

Stewart, Iain and John Lynch. *Earth: The Biography.* Washington, DC: National Geographic, 2008.

Suzuki, David. *The Sacred Balance.* Vancouver, BC: Greystone, 2002.

Taylor, Jill Bolte, Ph.D. *My Stroke of Insight.* New York: Penguin, 2006.

Thomas, Lewis. *The Lives of a Cell.* Toronto: Bantam, 1975.

Thoreau, Henry David. *Walden*. New York: Quality Paperback, 1997.

Tolle, Eckhart. *The Power of Now*. Novato, California: Namaste, 1999.

Watts, Alan. *The Way of Zen*. New York: Pantheon, 1957.

---. *Essence of Alan Watts*. Millbrae, California: Celestial Arts, 1977.

Wysession, Michael E., Ph.D. *How the Earth Works* - DVD and Course Guidebook. Chantilly, Virginia: The Teaching Co., 2008.

Zimmer, Carl. *Microcosm*. New York: Pantheon, 2008.

ENDNOTES

[1] *The American Heritage Dictionary of the English Language*, 4th Ed. (Boston: Houghton Mifflin, 2006).

[2] de Montaigne, Michel, 1500s.

[3] Robert Pirsig, *Zen and the Art of Motorcycle Maintenance* (New York: Bantam, 1974) 306.

[4] Dass, Ram. *Still Here* (New York: Penguin Putnam, 2000).

[5] Leonard Mlodinow, *The Drunkard's Walk* (New York: Pantheon, 2008) 173.

[6] Mlodinow 170.

[7] Mlodinow 189.

[8] Mlodinow 191.

[9] Guy Murchie, *The Seven Mysteries of Life* (Boston: Houghton Mifflin, 1981) 322-323.

[10] Jiri Langer, *Nine Gates to the Chassidic Mysteries*. (New York: Behrman House, 1976) 86.

[11] Annie Dillard, *Pilgrim at Tinker Creek* (Toronto: Bantam, 1974) 35.

[12] Michael E. Wysession, Ph.D., *How the Earth Works*, Course Guidebook (Chantilly, VA, The Teaching Company, 2008) 235.

[13] Anne Marie Helmenstine, "How Much are the Elements in your Body Worth?" (February 6, 2011).

[14] David Suzuki, *The Sacred Balance* (Vancouver, BC: Greystone, 2002) 36.

[15] Robert Ricklefs, *The Economy of Nature*, 4th Ed. (New York: W.H. Freeman, 1994) 5.

[16] Suzuki 37.

[17] Suzuki 37.

[18] Suzuki 37-38.

[19] Suzuki 38.

[20] Suzuki 51.

[21] Murchie 36-37.

[22] Jeffrey Bennett, Seth Shostak, Bruce Jakosky, *Life in the Universe* (San Francisco: Addison Wesley, 2003).

[23] Bennett, et. al. 91.

[24] Bennett, et. al. 95.

[25] Suzuki 66.

[26] Wysession 131.

[27] Suzuki 62.

[28] Jorge Luis Borges, "Poem of the Fourth Element," *Selected Poems* (A. Coleman Ed. New York: Penguin, 1999) 163.

[29] William Bryant Logan, *Dirt* (New York: W.W. Norton, 1995) 2.

[30] Logan 96.

[31] Logan 64-65.

[32] Logan 15.
[33] Logan 152
[34] Suzuki 101.
[35] Carl Zimmer, *Microcosm* (New York: Pantheon, 2008) 54.
[36] Suzuki 92.
[37] Logan 134.
[38] Iain Stewart and John Lynch, *Earth: The Biography* (Washington, DC: National Geographic, 2008) 136.
[39] Stewart and Lynch 136.
[40] Stephen Hawking, *A Brief History of Time* (New York: Bantam, 1988), 121-122.
[41] Matt Ridley, *Genome* (New York: Perennial, 1999) 40.
[42] Sean B Carroll, *Endless Forms Most Beautiful* (New York: W.W. Norton, 2005) 114.
[43] Sean B. Carroll, (*Scientific American*, "Regulating Evolution" (May 2008).
[44] Zimmer 29.
[45] Zimmer 74.
[46] Carroll 9.
[47] Katherine S. Pollard, *Scientific American*, "What Makes Us Human" (May 2009) 44-49.
[48] Pollard 49.
[49] Murchie 137.
[50] Ursula Goodenough, *The Sacred Depths of Nature* (Oxford, UK: Oxford University Press, 1998) 132-133.
[51] Ricklefs 263.
[52] Murchie 135.
[53] Ricklefs 262.
[54] Marcia Bjornerud, *Reading the Rocks* (Cambridge, MA: Westview, 2005) 19.
[55] Bjornerud 20.
[56] Wysession, Lecture One.
[57] Ricklefs 133.
[58] Suzuki 92.
[59] Ricklefs 169.
[60] Bennett, Shostak, Jakosky 64.
[61] Murchie 527.
[62] Goodenough 148.
[63] Goodenough 148.
[64] Goodenough 148.
[65] Don DeLillo, *White Noise*, (New York: Penguin, 1985) 228-229.
[66] Joel R. Primack and Nancy Ellen Abrams, *The View From the Center of the Universe* (New York: Riverhead, 2006) 151.
[67] Murchie 37.
[68] Murchie 37.

[69] Goodenough 28.
[70] Goodenough 34.
[71] Goodenough 49.
[72] Wysession, Lecture Four.
[73] Russell G. Foster and Leon Kreitzman, *Rhythms of Life* (New Haven: Yale University Press 2004) 2.
[74] Foster and Kreitzman 16.
[75] Foster and Kreitzman 15.
[76] Foster and Kreitzman 136-137.
[77] Foster and Kreitzman.
[78] Foster and Kreitzman.
[79] Edward Abbey, *Desert Solitaire* (New York: Ballantine, 1968).
[80] Bennett, Shostak, Jakosky 4-6.
[81] Primack and Abrams 115.
[82] Brian Cox and Andrew Cohen, *Wonders of the Universe* (New York: HarperCollins, 2011) 240.
[83] Cox & Cohen 240.
[84] William Least Heat-Moon, *Blue Highways* (Boston: Houghton Mifflin, 1982) 133.
[85] Murchie 497.
[86] Wysession, Lecture 26.
[87] Stewart & Lynch 31.
[88] Stewart & Lynch 47.
[89] Stewart & Lynch 39.
[90] Stewart & Lynch.
[91] Logan 9.
[92] Gary Snyder, *A Place in Space* (Washington, DC: Counterpoint, 1995) 184.
[93] Murchie 43.
[94] Murchie 46.
[95] Murchie 73.
[96] Murchie 47.
[97] Murchie 47.
[98] Murchie 48.
[99] Dillard 114.
[100] Murchie 74.
[101] Suzuki 142.
[102] John D. Barrow, *The Artful Universe Expanded* (Oxford, UK: Oxford University Press, 2005) 87.
[103] David Attenborough, *Life on Earth* (Boston: Little, Brown, 1979) 184-185.
[104] Pierre Gingras, *The Secret Lives of Birds* (Willowdale, Ontario, Canada: Firefly, 1997) 146.
[105] Gingras 147.
[106] Gingras 72.

[107] Attenborough 173.
[108] Attenborough 173.
[109] Gingras 101.
[110] Gingras.
[111] Attenborough.
[112] William Least Heat-Moon, *Prairy Erth* (Boston: Houghton Mifflin, 1991) 116.
[113] Loren Eiseley, *The Immense Journey* (New York: Vintage, 1953).
[114] Murchie 47.
[115] Henry David Thoreau, *Walden* (New York: Quality Paperback, 1997).
[116] Osho, *The Spiritual Path* (Lewes, UK: Ivy Press, 2007) 35.
[117] Alan Watts, *The Way of Zen* (New York: Pantheon, 1957).
[118] Alan Watts, *Essence of Alan Watts* (Millbrae, CA: Celestial Arts, 1977).
[119] Eckhart Tolle, *The Power of Now,* (Novato, CA: Namaste, 1999) 50.
[120] Tolle 49-50.
[121] Mary Oliver. "Wild Geese," *New and Selected Poems, Volume One,* (Boston: Beacon, 1992) 110.
[122] Cox and Cohen 136.
[123] Cox and Cohen 135.
[124] Primack and Abrams 94.
[125] Primack and Abams 97.
[126] Primack and Abrams 98.
[127] Primack and Abrams 98.
[128] Logan 7.
[129] Primack and Abrams.
[130] Italo Calvino, *Cosmicomics* (San Diego: Harcourt Brace Jovanovich, 1965) 46-47.
[131] Julia Cameron, *The Artist's Way* (New York: Penguin Putnam, 1992) 110.
[132] Dillard 9-10.
[133] Dillard 81.
[134] Dillard 35.
[135] Dillard 81.
[136] Jack Kornfield, *Buddha's Little Instruction Book* (New York: Bantam, 1994) 17.
[137] Kornfield 58.
[138] Leary, Timothy, Informal talk at Rice University, ~1967.
[139] Dillard 80.
[140] Dillard 11-12.
[141] Murchie 345.
[142] Murchie 351.
[143] Murchie 351.
[144] Murchie.356-357.
[145] Murchie 359.
[146] Murchie 359.

[147] Primack and Abrams.

[148] Osho 352.

[149] Suzuki 140.

[150] Lewis Thomas, *The Lives of a Cell* (Toronto: Bantam, 1975) 86.

[151] Thomas 84.

[152] Suzuki 140.

[153] Jeanette Norden, Ph.D., *Understanding the Brain*, Course Guidebook (Chantilly, VA: The Teaching Co., 2007) 97.

[154] Steven Johnson, *Mind Wide Open* (New York: Scribner, 2004) 29.

[155] Norden, Lecture 10.

[156] Johnson 61.

[157] Norden, Course Guidebook 113-114.

[158] Jill Bolte Taylor, Ph.D., *My Stroke of Insight* (New York: Penguin, 2006) 17.

[159] Norden 97.

[160] Johnson 154.

[161] Ed Diener and Robert Biswas-Diener, *Happiness* (Malden, MA: Blackwell, 2008).

[162] Johnson 137.

[163] Johnson 138.

[164] Johnson 138.

[165] Palmer, George, Informal conversation, 2012.

[166] Norden, Lecture 13.

[167] Norden, Lecture 13.

[168] Norden, Lecture 14.

[169] Norden, Lecture 14.

[170] Tim Friend, *Animal Talk* (New York: Free Press, 2004).

[171] Friend 120-121.

[172] Friend 128.

[173] David V. Smith and Robert F. Margolskee, *Scientific American*, "Making Sense of Taste" (March 18, 2001).

[174] Primack and Abrams.

[175] Suzuki 130.

[176] Fritjof Capra, *The Tao of Physics*, (New York: Bantam, 1975) 276.

[177] Robert S.deRopp, *The Warrior's Way* (New York: Dell, 1979) 302.

Made in the USA
Lexington, KY
20 September 2014